Maynooth Studies in Local His

Wise-woman of Kildare

Moll Anthony and popular tradition in the east of Ireland

Erin Kraus

FOUR COURTS PRESS

Set in 10pt on 12pt Bembo by
Carrigboy Typesetting Services for
FOUR COURTS PRESS LTD
7 Malpas Street, Dublin 8, Ireland
www.fourcourtspress.ie
and in North America for
FOUR COURTS PRESS
c/o ISBS, 920 N.E. 58th Avenue, Suite 300, Portland, OR 97213.

ISBN 978-1-84682-292-6

Printed in England by
Antony Rowe Ltd, Chippenham, Wilts.

Contents

Acknowledgments

During the course of my research and writing for the thesis on which this small book is based, a number of individuals and institutions provided invaluable assistance and encouragement. First, I would like to thank my MA supervisor at NUI Galway, Dr Lillis Ó Laoire, for his guidance throughout the entire process, and his continuing support of my research. Also, I must express my gratitude towards Dr Louis de Paor and Dr Nessa Cronin, both of the Irish Studies programme at NUI Galway, for their enthusiasm for the project from the outset. The staff at the James Hardiman library at NUI Galway also could not have been more helpful, and I extend special thanks to the staff in Special Collections.

I am also deeply indebted to the staff of the Folklore Department at University College Dublin. They were incredibly helpful and knowledgeable, which made navigating the manuscript collections that much easier, and my time spent there a pleasure. For a great kindness in a stressful period of the project, I would also like to thank Mr Phil Murphy, the current editor of the periodical, *Ireland's Own*. He was so kind as to track down articles and mail them to me, and I greatly appreciated his assistance.

I would also like to thank my mother, Elissa Kraus, and Sean Fabun for reading through drafts of this book and helping me to iron out the little things. Finally, I extend my deepest gratitude to my close friends and family, who have encouraged me from the beginning, and continue to be a source of love and support.

1. Introduction: understanding tradition and the mythical landscape

Many years [ago] a party of men were returning home from Naas Cinema to Kill, late at night. A few miles outside the town, they encountered a Banshee who was sitting on the side of the road combing her golden tresses. One of the men who was of a humorous nature made a bet with the others that he would take the comb. He then dismounted from the bicycle, and went towards the 'fairywoman', and took the comb from her hands. He mounted his machine again and rejoined his companions but the Banshee followed him in a vain endeavour to retrieve her comb. At last he reached his house, but she sat on the window and broke panes of glass. He then gave her the comb, and she disappeared, but every night after that she visited the house, and soon afterwards the man died.[1]

TRADITION VERSUS MODERNITY?

For generations the Irish people have lamented the loss of their traditional culture, the fading of their native language, practices and beliefs. As Diarmuid Ó Giolláin writes: 'The death – and the protection – of tradition has been a common theme in Irish cultural life up to the present day. The death of traditions in general cannot be doubted, any more than the birth of new traditions.'[2] It is undoubtedly true that Ireland has changed greatly, seemingly with increasing rapidity. Change accelerated from the turn of the 19th century by the erosion of the Irish vernacular, the spread of institutionalized education, the increasing power of the church, the trend towards urbanization and industrialization, and population decline due to famine and emigration. What is less certain is exactly how many traditions have actually been lost, and how many have simply changed so that they are not as easily recognizable. Ó Giolláin seems to suggest in the preceding statements that the loss of tradition is in fact very black and white – some traditions 'die' while others are 'born.' As he clarifies later on, however, the process is not that straightforward. The story of the banshee presented at the beginning of this introduction provides some insight into the process by which traditions change. By mentioning both the magic of tradition and the magic of modernity together, this narrative provides some insight into the complexity of the processes of tradition and change.

It has long been argued that modern society is by nature antithetical to cultural traditions: that the modern and the traditional are mutually exclusive and cannot exist side by side.[3] This story of the banshee, however, collected in the 1930s, suggests that this is not necessarily true. Although the teller relates that this confrontation with the supernatural occurred 'many years [ago]', the party of men are returning late at night not from a pub or *céilí* house, but from a cinema. Also unusual, they are not walking the dark roads, but are instead riding bicycles. Contrary to the idea that the modern must necessarily collide with and take the place of tradition, the modern elements within this story blend seamlessly into the narrative. It is merely the peripheral details of the story that isolate this narrative from the larger corpus of death-messenger legends. In fact, the core of this story remains so similar to other banshee legends that it is difficult to separate it from the others at all.[4] It very closely follows the pattern of the most common of the banshee interference legends identified by Patricia Lysaght, labelled 'the comb legend'. Following the pattern of the A-redaction, a young man takes the comb from the fairy woman for sport, after which she follows him home and sits at his window, breaking the panes of glass. The man eventually gives her back her comb, but she haunts him every night following the encounter, and he soon dies.[5]

This is but one example of the blending of modernity and tradition within Irish culture, a phenomenon that is more prevalent than those who claim modernity 'kills' tradition might expect.[6] While it may appear as if Irish tradition has been diluted and diffused over time, it also seems evident that certain core beliefs persist unchanged. Such is the case with this banshee legend, a narrative that is the product of a community removed from the Irish-speaking, rural, western communities that are most often associated with tradition. Collected in the town of Naas in Co. Kildare, this story shows the effects of Anglicization, language shift, urbanization, and industrialization – it was collected in the English language, takes place outside of a town, and includes the modern inventions of the cinema and the bicycle. Can it be said, however, that this is not a traditional story because it contains non-traditional elements? Does the process of modernity, and its effects on society, necessarily doom tradition?

Ó Giolláin argues: 'The continuity of traditional cultural elements is not necessarily compromised by embracing rather than resisting modernity, even if the resulting "second life" may not satisfy the purist.'[7] This seems a valid, if unpopular, argument. If the core remains the same, does the introduction of modern elements affect the authenticity of the tradition? When one considers that cultural change is a constant process, the idea that it should not affect authenticity becomes more plausible. Change does not necessarily constitute a diminishing of tradition, but a resurfacing – just as the surface of the landscape changes over time while the essence of earth does not change. It is a living, mutable world, and in the same way it is a living tradition.[8]

Folk tradition is not a static body from the past handed down from generation to generation intact. It has lived through centuries of change, has endured countless invasions of men, disease, learning and religion. Through all this, it has adapted and changed, sometimes quickly and sometimes so slowly that the change is not registered. With the advent of modernity and the increasing speed of change, the death-knell has been sounded for Irish traditions many times. However, a living tradition cannot really be lost. Elements and figures that were once prominent may seemingly disappear, but often they simply hide beneath new added layers of tradition. By no means does this imply that traditions never disappear completely. This idea simply suggests that more tradition may survive than is at first apparent; oftentimes it is only necessary to look in unexpected places, at unexpected sources.

LOOKING OUTSIDE THE WEST

A first step towards rediscovering hidden traditions would be to expand the focus of study to include areas outside of the western and northern fringes of Ireland. Too often have these places been forgotten and ignored, their cultural significance undervalued. Because the east is associated with Anglicization and urbanization, those seeking the 'real Ireland' – both scholars and tourists – often bypass it in favour of more 'authentic' communities to the west.[9] However, by often literally speeding through the east, most people do not engage with the landscape and so the cultural significance of the land and the people who live there is not understood, and often discounted.[10] Figures 1 to 3 illustrate the geographic area on which this study concentrates, and provide a demonstration of the mythical landscape of the area. One type of tradition that constitutes a significant piece of Irish culture is *dindshenchas*, or place-lore: collections of narratives and histories that give significance to the land. M.M. Bakhtin writes that in places of great significance, which he calls chronotopes, 'time, as it were, thickens, takes on flesh, becomes artistically visible; likewise, space becomes charged and responsive to the movements of time, plot and history'.[11] In this way, it could be said that the past and present exist side by side – that those of history and myth inhabit the landscape of the present. Consequently, if the time is not taken to engage with the landscape, to learn its stories, then the traditions that lie beneath the veil of modernity may be missed.

This is especially true regarding the area within the Pale, the circle of safety around Dublin that supposedly kept the native Irish at bay. It is perhaps thought to be the most unlikely place to find authentic traditions such as the retelling of place-lore. In her study of banshee legend, Patricia Lysaght points out that in the eastern province of Leinster: 'there has been only very occasional collecting activity by full-time or part-time [folklore] collectors'.[12] The

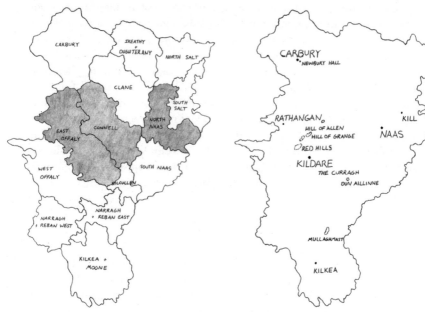

1 Map of the baronies of Co. Kildare   2 Map of the geography of Co. Kildare

3 Map of the mythological landscape of Co. Kildare

vibrancy and many-layered nature of the lore surrounding even one small landmark in the east seems to indicate that the lack of focus on its tradition is unfounded. Among the records of the Schools' Manuscript Collection held at University College Dublin there are three brief references to a single hill that lies not 30 miles from Dublin city centre, just north-east of Kildare town.[13] The information in each is given in a straightforward manner, devoid of the life often found in folktales, and in a bare-bones form that many would see as the result of the dilution of tradition. Beneath their bleak exteriors, however, lies a complex layering of folk beliefs and traditions.

The descriptions in the narratives are very similar: at the top of a nearby hill there is a cave that no one enters or disturbs.[14] Though a simple statement, the unspoken prohibition against interference with the cave in any way suggests that the local people have connected the cave to the supernatural in some way. This idea is confirmed by the third story, which says, 'People have often heard the sound of music in it.'[15] Music heard in a hillside cave suggests that this is the spot of a fairy rath, or dwelling place. However, the legend, as it may be called, anchored at this landmark is more complex than a case of fairy residence, for two of the stories also say that a white calf emerges from the cave every seven years, and anyone who grabs its tail will be dragged back into the cave to be held forever. The reference to a white cow then connects this place to Irish mother and fertility goddesses, who are often described as taking the forms of cows. Yet another layer of tradition is added, however, when the name given to the landmark in all three stories is noted – 'the Witch's Cave'. One of the stories also describes, not the form of a cow emerging from the cave, but that of a witch. It is possible that the fairy queen or goddess within the cave could have been reduced to the title of witch over time. However, it is also possible that the name came from another, mortal source. In more recent times, an unusual woman who lived in the area could have been labelled a witch. In this way, one small landmark illustrates the overlapping and layering of myth and history that creates and adds significance to the landscape. These brief, stark accounts suggest an incredibly rich interweaving of goddess mythology, fairy lore, and folk legend that adds credence to the idea that the east deserves to be reexamined and its traditions reevaluated.

MOLL ANTHONY, WISE-WOMAN OF KILDARE

The story does not end with the cave at the top of the hill, however. This particular hill, known as the Hill of Grange, was once the home of the wise-woman and healer, Moll Anthony, stories of whom have been told across Ireland. Dáithí Ó hÓgáin lists Moll and Biddy Early as the two most well known wise-women in Ireland, and yet, Moll has been largely ignored by scholars, bypassed for women like her in the west and north.[16] Sir Walter

Fitzgerald researched and wrote an article on Moll in 1915 for the *Journal of the Kildare Archaeological Society*, but very rarely has she been mentioned by other scholars, even when writing particularly about wise-women.[17] Gearóid Ó Crualaoich's definitive book on the wise-woman healer, *The book of the Cailleach: stories of the wise-woman healer*, focuses mostly on narratives about Munster women.[18] He particularly notes that he will not deal with stories about the most famous of the wise-women, Biddy Early, but he makes no mention of Moll. There has also been a good deal of research done on Biddy, including Meda Ryan's, *Biddy Early: the wise-woman of Clare*, and Eddie Lenihan's, *Biddy Early*. Ryan does mention Moll Anthony, relating a story about her that Biddy told throughout her life, but she does nothing more than provide the story. All other scholarly references to Moll are brief, usually relying on Fitzgerald's account if written after 1915.

When Moll Anthony's individual cultural significance is considered, the lack of attention paid to her seems strange, particularly since her legend is located in an English-speaking community within the Pale. For this very reason Moll Anthony is significant in her own right, not only for the layers of traditions that contribute to her character, but also for her representation of undervalued or ignored traditions in the east. In order to best exhibit her own cultural merit, as well as that of her community, an examination of her stories and the cultural context in which they were formed and are told is important. In this way, the various layers of tradition that form her character can be separated and identified, thereby revealing the richness of traditions in the area. Therefore, Moll Anthony provides an excellent case for the re-evaluation of the persistence of legend traditions and their associated beliefs in the east.

SOURCES AND METHODS

The material used to examine the character of Moll Anthony consists mainly of a corpus of stories regarding her life and legend. From a variety of sources, 30 stories were collected for this study, 24 of which directly reference Moll Anthony, while the remaining six make possible indirect reference to her. The majority of the stories are from manuscript material collected by the Irish Folklore Commission and held at University College Dublin. Among the stories that directly reference Moll, seven were found in the Main Manuscript Collection and an additional two were found in the Schools' Manuscript Collection. One story was collected from a 19th-century published source, and twelve from 20th-century published sources. An additional two published stories were derived from the Fitzgerald article previously mentioned. The publication, *Ireland's Own*, was the source of many of the published stories, while books account for the rest. All six of the stories that make indirect reference to Moll were found in the Schools' Manuscript Collection. It was possible to determine the source location of 23 of the stories, all but one of which were collected in Leinster.[19]

This book is organized so that each layer of tradition that contributes to Moll's character is examined independently, with connections being drawn between the traditions throughout. The first chapter, therefore, will discuss fairy belief in Ireland and among the community surrounding Moll's home. It will then examine the origin story of Moll's powers in relation to fairy belief and local tradition. The second chapter will then examine the application of fairy belief in Moll's particular case, by exploring the practice of folk medicine, ideas about natural and supernatural illness, and the various methods for curing. Throughout the chapter, stories of Moll's cures will be examined within this context. Finally, the third chapter will look at some of the traditions of female power that also are layered into the character of Moll. The archetypes of the wise-woman and the *cailleach* will be addressed, as well as Moll's connection to mother goddesses such as Bóand and Brigit. This demystifying of Moll Anthony will ultimately be used as a case for the re-evaluation of tradition in the eastern counties of Ireland.

2. Fairy woman: belief in the supernatural

To their astonishment on reaching the road they found the coffin where they had laid it down, and the strangers nowhere to be seen. Then, acting on their mother's advice, they brought the coffin to the house. The Widow Anthony, noticing that the lid was not screwed down, told them to raise it, and inside they saw 'a grand slip of a gerrel' lying as if she was asleep; the colour was in her cheeks, and the warmth in her body.[1]

Christy Hickey, on how Moll Anthony came to Mullaghmast

'AWAY WITH THE FAIRIES'

Moll Anthony was a woman veiled in mystery during her life and remains so now, long after her death. Her exceptional abilities to understand the world around her, to negotiate the unknown, and to heal the miseries of countless individuals engendered both fear and respect among those who knew of her. Her abilities, however, meant that she did not easily fit into the natural world – she could not comfortably be explained by natural laws. Consequently, she was often associated with the supernatural. The connections drawn between her character and the Otherworld were not consistent, however. Some believed that she was influenced by demons, while others thought she was in communication with the fairies. The varying interpretations of Moll's supernatural connections seem to have depended on the larger belief systems of the individuals telling the stories. Therefore, in order to better understand the many-layered character of Moll Anthony, it is important to understand the folk belief systems followed among the Irish population in general, and within Moll's own community in particular.

The study of belief is a difficult one: it is very rare that informants or other resources explain what is believed and what is not. Fortunately, where belief is not explained, there are sources from which belief may be inferred. David J. Hufford writes: 'The natural vehicle of folk belief, perhaps of most belief, is stories that show what is true by what is said to have happened.'[2] Stories, therefore, provide a glimpse of the ideas and practices that constitute both the teller's and the traditional audience's belief system – the totality of their supernatural beliefs, including both popular and institutionalized religious influences. The stories, in fact, describe the world as seen and understood by the teller, by explaining his or her connection to the land, detailing the known environment (the natural) and the unknown (the supernatural). Angela Bourke writes that the stories 'deepen the native's knowledge of her physical surroundings, but also thriftily use the gaps in the known environment for the elaboration of an imagined world where all the things that are in Heaven and Earth and yet not dreamt of in rational philosophy may be accommodated'.[3] In this way, things that cannot be explained by the natural world are given supernatural explanations by those trying to understand their environment.

The following narrative provides an example of this process: a farmer walking across a field was suddenly cut off by ditches that opened up in the ground and grew wider as he tried to jump across them. The teller finishes the story by saying, 'People say there are fairies in that field.'[4] Although the teller does not explicitly attribute this occurrence to supernatural causes, his mention of fairies in the field provides an implicit explanation for it. It is stories such as this one that provide valuable insight into the belief systems of the Irish people. Much research has been done on fairy belief in particular, by such well-known folklorists and antiquarians as Lady Wilde, Lady Gregory, William Butler Yeats, and W.Y. Evans Wentz.[5] From their works, as well as other scholarly sources, a general knowledge about fairy belief in Ireland can be gained.

For local studies in Moll's community, however, there are other sources that prove valuable. One of Lady Augusta Gregory's informants claimed 'all the people in Kildare believe in them [fairies].'[6] It is important, however, to determine to what extent this was actually true. The Schools' Manuscript Collection held at University College Dublin is a valuable asset for determining the local existence of fairy belief. The collection consists of folklore material collected by 11-to-14 year-old primary school students in the period 1937–8, and is separated in volumes by school, parish, barony, and county, so that specific areas may be examined. The local material on supernatural belief to be examined here was collected from the parishes of Allen, Naas, and Rathangan, all in close proximity to the Hill of Grange. The material available from just these three parishes was surprisingly rich, as stories and information regarding fairies, banshees, ghosts, holy wells, and healers was plentiful. By looking at these stories, at the information collected by the children, it is possible to ascertain to some degree the beliefs about the supernatural that were held by these people in the period leading up to at least 1938. The information collected makes it quite clear that a belief in fairies was quite active even up until this period.[7]

FAIRY BELIEF IN IRELAND

The forms that the supernatural take in folktales and stories differ considerably, across both space and time, depending on the larger belief system of the people concerned. Hufford defines folk belief in his article on the supernatural: 'Folk beliefs – unofficial beliefs – are those that develop and operate outside powerful social structures.'[8] However, while folk belief played a large part in people's lives, institutionalized religion often played a significant part as well. Because of varying degrees of blending and mixing of these two sources of belief, ideas about the supernatural in Ireland are vast and varied. Change has also occurred over time due to the eroding of the Irish vernacular, the spread of institutionalized education, the increasing power of the church, the development of urbanization, and the loss of people to famine and emigration. For a time, it was believed that this process was so devastating that all Irish traditions would be lost. Writing during the Great Famine, Sir William Wilde, the doctor and antiquarian, wrote of all of these degrading factors: 'Together with the rapid decay of the Irish vernacular, in which most of our legends, romantic tales, ballads, and bardic annals, the vestiges of Pagan rites, and the relics of fairy charms were preserved – can superstition, or if [not] superstitious belief, can superstitious practice continue to exist?'[9] Expressing the loss of stories, practices, and beliefs due to the loss of so many people, Wilde also wrote that the fairies themselves were leaving, migrating to the western fringes of the island before leaving its shores entirely. However, Moll Anthony and the legends of fairies that surround her are proof that complex folk beliefs and practices survived, even within the Pale.

A large portion of the folk beliefs that survived pertained to the figures of fairies, or 'the good people'. Even with the spread of more Romanized Catholicism and the increase in the influence of the church in Ireland the belief in the existence of these supernatural beings continued.[10] Although ideas about them sometimes changed, many old beliefs still remained. The old stories continue to be told, and new experiences produce new stories that parallel them. Dermot MacManus's book, *The middle kingdom*, adds some support to this claim, professing to be 'the only collection of true Irish fairy tales'.[11] Published in 1959, the collection includes stories told by primary witnesses to supernatural events, or contact with the fairies, illustrating that, not only did the stories survive, but the beliefs as well.

However, trying to determine the form of these beliefs is often more complex than determining that they are still active. Because fairy traditions have existed for so long, and have seen so many changes, there is a great deal of variation among the stories about them, pertaining to their origins, hierarchies, appearance, habitation, powers and so on. Old ideas mingle with new, and Christian with pagan, creating a complicated blending of stories that is impossible to untangle. What is generally acknowledged, however, is that 'the good people' occupy a sort of middle world, or Middle Kingdom, as MacManus calls it, between the human world and the divine.[12] Describing this very fact, the Revd John O'Hanlon wrote in 1870: 'Fairies are generally thought, by the peasantry, to partake of a mixed human and spiritual nature'.[13] In this way, their physical beings are thought to be a combination of material and spiritual, just as the world they live in is thought to exist somewhere between Heaven and Earth.

The reasons for their existence in this middle world, their stories of origin, fall into a number of schools of thought. Before the influence of the church altered people's ideas about the origins of the fairy races it was often believed that the succession of ancient races in Ireland were the source of the various supernatural populations. Lady Wilde points out that the Book of Lismore names as the origin the Tuatha de Danann, or the Tribes of Danu, one ancient race of beautiful, heroic people who occupied Ireland before the human Milesians came and forced them underground. Similarly, the Book of Armagh names the origins of the different fairy races as all the ancient conquered races that had been forced into existence in the Middle Kingdom and had become 'the gods of the earth'.[14] It was believed that these ancient people, or the spirits of their dead, occupied the hills, mountains and caves of Ireland and acted as earth spirits, pagan gods and goddesses, or at least demi-gods.[15]

Over time, however, the more earthly, pagan origins were combined with origin stories influenced by church teachings. Although the old ideas were not completely forgotten, these new ideas became more popular. According to K.M. Briggs, most of the informants she interviewed believed that fairies were the spirits of the dead, remaining on earth for a while until they make their way to Heaven.[16] Briggs also reported that many people believe that the fairies 'are too bad for Heaven, but too good for Hell; they are in the middle way between men and angels'.[17] This in-between existence is explained by the expulsion of angels from Heaven by God. Those who landed on the earth and sea stayed and built their domains there, living in relative peace with humans. Those who landed in Hell, however, were placed under the control of the devil, and were sent back to earth to torment the people. The appearances of all three 'races' of fairies reflected these positions as well; those of land and sea were beautiful while those of Hell were tiny and ugly creatures.[18]

In all cases, the existence of the fairies in this middle world meant that they, and those connected with them, could not be entirely understood, and so they demanded respect and often fear. The unpredictability of 'the good people' was well known, and was another source of fear. Bourke writes: 'They share space and time with the human population, but they use both differently.'[19] Because of this, it was never known when one's path would cross with a fairy or other supernatural being. All that could be done was to recognize patterns in their appearance and contact with the human world. Reflecting this, the stories most often describe them being seen on the borders of both space and time. Bourke describes this trend: 'People encounter them on the boundaries: either in space – between townlands or on beaches between high and low tide; or in time – at dusk or at midnight; on Hallowe'en or May Eve.'[20] It is for this reason that not everyone can see them, and when they do, exactly what people see varies greatly.[21]

The great diversity of description among even first-hand accounts of supernatural sightings makes it nearly impossible to organize them in any semblance of order. As Lysaght writes: 'Any attempt to categorize supernatural beings is fraught with difficulties and uncertainties. Something which by its very nature is mystical, dim and vague cannot readily be fitted into a logical system.'[22] Nevertheless, at one time there was a large, complicated hierarchy of beings within the Irish supernatural world. Fairies were grouped into tribes governed by kings and queens, reflecting the social order of their human contemporaries. As the human world changed, however, the stories of the fairy courts were increasingly forgotten, and different images of supernatural beings came to the fore. Individual spirits who had once had names and territories were combined into groups, and their names and histories were lost. Often they were simply divided into 'good' and 'bad', depending on where they landed when they were tossed from Heaven. As the stories were forgotten, attitudes towards the supernatural began to change. What was once regarded with fear and awe was reduced to wonderful, and then further reduced to benign romantic figures. Though once regarded with caution and wariness by people within the tradition, with questioning or increasing disbelief respect gave way to curiosity or disdain. For those outside the tradition, supernatural beings were lifted out of context as objects of curiosity devoid of their awful power. Susan Stewart calls this change of opinion towards the supernatural the 'domestication' of the fairy.[23]

An example of this is the changing opinions about the size of supernatural beings. Once thought to have been of human or super-human proportions, increasingly over time they were viewed as diminutive in stature, more cute than fear inspiring. Stewart writes of this: 'Although the fairies described before 1594 do not seem to be particularly diminutive, it is the convention by the late Renaissance in England to depict them as miniature human beings.'[24] The once-proud fairy courtiers riding white horses and clothed in gold and other finery, were reduced to miniature sprites, more natural than supernatural in that they often physically resembled their natural surroundings. During the Victorian period, however, and especially during the Celtic revival in Ireland, medieval texts were rediscovered and the image of regal fairy courts was revived. However, these revived fairies lacked the powerful vitality of earlier images: what was once a source of fear was now a source of delight. For example, Lady Wilde describes the fairy court in the following manner:

> The fairies of the earth are small and beautiful. They passionately love music and dancing, and live luxuriously in their palaces under the hills and deep in the mountain caves … The fairy king and princes dress in green, with red caps bound on the head with a golden fillet. The fairy queen and the great court ladies are robed in glittering silver gauze, spangled with diamonds, and their long golden hair sweeps the ground as they dance on the greensward.[25]

Although images of the fairies have changed over time, distinctions between 'trooping' and solitary fairies seem fairly consistent. 'Trooping' fairies are those that live together in large communities or tribes under the guidance of royal members. They are usually connected to a particular rath or territory and are usually thought to be of human or super-human proportions (although this changed over time as previously discussed). They are often described as beautiful and ageless, and stories of their interactions with local human populations are numerous. Solitary fairies, on the other hand, often do not belong to these tribes, and wander the wilds alone. They can be beautiful or hideous, of large or small stature, although some types of solitary fairies, such as the leprechauns, are almost always said to be diminutive. Banshees, pookas, leprechauns and brownies, along with countless others, fit into this category.[26]

Despite the varying appearances and behaviour of the fairies, they were always dealt with respectfully, or a person risked incurring their anger or disapproval. Nora Naughton writes: 'Fairies were generally given positive or complimentary titles and, as a protective measure to guard against their potential anger, never criticized.'[27] It is for this reason that the fairies are usually referred to as 'the good people' or 'the gentry'. As Bourke points out, there were strict codes of behaviour for interaction with the fairies, and the stories and traditions surrounding them often describe the consequences of happening upon them and breaking the codes of behaviour. Often, the fairies showed displeasure with human interference by upsetting things within the house, stealing the butter, or causing animals to fall sick. More severe punishments for trespassing into fairy matters included sickness and physical abuse towards humans. When thorn trees were cut down, or houses were built on fairy paths, the perpetrators could expect these relatively minor inconveniences. One schoolboy from Moll's community wrote: 'The old people told me about a man's arm going powerless from cutting down a certain tree. There was a man cutting down a fairy tree and he shivered to death.'[28] The boy also claims, however, that he had cut a fishing rod out of a rath and had remained unharmed. A young girl from the same area provides some advice to protect oneself from fairy malevolence: 'If an evil spirit pursues you at night, make for a running stream. If you can cross it you will be safe.'[29] Advice such as this would have been taken very seriously, as many interactions between the fairies and the human world were more sinister than these minimal punishments.

A large body of Irish fairy lore is dedicated to stories of fairy kidnappings: unexplained disappearances and sudden sicknesses, with fairy changelings left in a loved one's place. Patrick Logan identifies the groups of people traditionally kidnapped by the fairies.[30] Most numerous among the tales are the stories of the exchange of changelings for beautiful human infants. Often accompanied by the sound of a strong wind or a swarm of bees, a once healthy infant is replaced by a wrinkled, old-faced, cranky creature that often does not resemble the healthy infant at all. In other instances, women who have recently

given birth are kidnapped to care for fairy children, or midwives are snatched
to assist at fairy deliveries. Handsome young men and pretty young women
are taken as fairy husbands and brides, and talented musicians, poets, and
athletes are kidnapped to entertain fairy courts. O'Hanlon writes of the pipers
taken: 'These sons of melody, until almost dead with fatigue, are kept engaged
in furnishing music to finely-dressed, frisky little gentlemen and ladies.'[31] As
this observation indicates, those kidnapped by the fairies did sometimes come
back, although they were often greatly changed. Another instance of fairy-
human interaction concerns a group of female fairies known as the *leannán sí*,
the fairy lover. In these cases, a fairy woman takes a fancy to or falls in love
with a young human man, and he is helpless to resist her. She often stays with
him for a while, even marries and has his children, and then returns to her
home when she gets tired of him or he is no longer young.[32] The mortal man
is not necessarily hurt by this interaction, but he does not really have a choice
in the matter once she decides that he will be hers.

Finally, and most important for Moll's story, the fairies sometimes reward
those that they have taken advantage of, or borrowed for a time, by giving gifts
of both a material and non-material nature. Sometimes, musicians are rewarded
with a song or a new instrument, and midwives given money for their work.
According to one local schoolchild, a woman in the area who was said to be
'in communication with the fairies', woke up every morning to find some of
her chores done for her.[33] Concerning the kidnapping and release of young
women, Lady Wilde relates this tale:

> There they kept them for seven years, and at the end of that time, when
> they grew old and ugly, they were sent back, for the fairies love nothing
> so much as youth and beauty. But as a compensation for the slight put
> on them, the women were taught all the fairy secrets and the magical
> mystery that lies in herbs, and the strange power they have over diseases.
> So by this means the women became all-powerful, and by their charms
> or spells or potions could kill or save as they chose.[34]

As a result of stories such as this one, and a firm belief that such things did
occur, those who had special powers, or an uncanny ability to heal or know
another person's mind, were thought to have been 'away' for a time – with
the fairies – who then gave them this special knowledge. Such was the case
with Moll Anthony.

MOLL ANTHONY AND THE FAIRIES

The source of Moll Anthony's powers has been attributed to many things.
Some of the stories claim she was in communication with the devil.[35] The

majority associate her ability to cure with her interactions with the fairies: 'It was said she was in league with the fairies, and they charmed her with cures',[36] or that her 'almost supernatural ability to heal' was a 'gift obtained, it was thought, by the aid of "the Good People" or the Fairies'.[37] Among the 30 stories to be examined here, however, only three relate a detailed account of the origins of her powers, and two are written using the third as a source. For this reason, only the original version of this story will be examined, as the other two stories are nearly identical.[38] The source of this story is Fitzgerald's article in the *Journal of the Kildare Archaeological Society*, at the end of which he relates a story told to him by a local man, Christy Hickey, about the source of Moll's powers. As Fitzgerald points out, Hickey moves the location of the story to his own area, that of Mullaghmast.[39] However, this discrepancy could also be accounted for by the blending of two stories. This tale is unique, and is an intriguing account of Moll's early life, but it is certainly possible that the story relates to another woman entirely, and was only attached to Moll's legend later on.

Hickey relates the existence of a Widow Anthony in Mullaghmast, who sent her two sons out to a neighbouring field to tend some sheep. On their way there, they came across a funeral – four men carrying a coffin in a 'bearer'. As was the custom in the locality, they turned and followed the funeral, each taking a turn carrying the coffin. When they reached their mother's front door, they went inside to tell her the news, and then turned to leave again to tend to the sheep. They were astonished, however, to find the coffin lying in the road in front of the house with no one to be seen. The Widow Anthony bid them bring the coffin inside, and upon noticing that the lid was not nailed shut, they lifted it, and found a young girl looking very much alive. They revived her, and not knowing who she was, she remained with them in the household. When they were old enough, the older brother married her, and they had three children. One day, Mary, as they had called her, asked to accompany her husband to a local fair that she had never before attended. Upon his agreeing, they set off, and it was not long before they bought the filly he had needed. The man who sold him the filly, however, would not stop staring at Mary, and he claimed that she looked exactly like the daughter he had buried years before. His wife asked if they could retire to another room, and answering her, Mary said, 'Mother, there is no need, for I still have the strawberry mark on my arm.'[40] It was soon determined that the day of their daughter's funeral was the very day that Mary had been left at the Widow Anthony's doorstep.[41]

This story is exceptional for several reasons. First, the image of fairy funerals is a popular one in folk tradition, and there are innumerable stories of human encounters with them. This incident, however, is a bit different from most. In general, humans are not allowed to see, let alone partake in, fairy funerals – even when the body in the coffin is human, such as in this case. Most people are stopped on the road unexpectedly, unable to move, for no apparent reason. Naughton relates an incident in which a man's bicycle stopped unexpectedly, and he could not make it go forward. Badly frightened, the next day the man consults his priest, who informs him, 'There was something you weren't meant to see. There was something crossing the road.'[42] Also, Mary's funeral takes place during the day, when most fairy funerals are said to take place at night.

Of course, the most exceptional part of this story is that Mary is brought back from the dead. Her parents clearly remember her funeral, and yet the Widow Anthony and her sons revived her the same day after strange men had deposited her coffin at their doorstep. It appears that she was not simply revived, but was in fact brought back from death by supernatural beings that disappeared after leaving her in the road. The tradition of the revival of the seemingly dead is prevalent in Irish folklore, as explained by Ilana Harlow. She provides numerous examples of similar stories. However, in nearly all of them, the revived individual is a source of fear – an element that does not appear in the story of Mary's revival.[43] There is no mention of fear whatsoever, not even when the truth of her revival is revealed at the end. Also strange, although she reanimates within her coffin, she is never thought to be a ghost, and is immediately recognized as being alive. For such extraordinary occurrences, the reaction of those involved within the story is remarkably subdued.

There are traces of folk belief and tradition hidden within the story that are not explained, but instead are assumed to be understood. For example, the strange men are never called supernatural, but they disappear and do not act as humans would, leaving a coffin on the side of the road. Also, the recognition, at the end of the story, that Mary was buried and revived in one day indicates that she was 'away.' It is unclear, however, whether the intention of the fairies was to revive her from the dead, or if they had planned to kidnap the seemingly dead girl and were thwarted by the boys' morally correct behaviour. It is entirely possible that, because the boys followed the coffin and showed respect for the dead, they saved the girl from capture.[44] The strawberry mark on her shoulder is another indication of her involvement with the supernatural, as those who had dealings with 'the good people', or the devil for that matter, were often thought to be physically marked in such a way. This strange tale of a girl brought back from the dead by the fairies, therefore, explains the supernatural powers attributed to her later in life. As explained earlier, those who were taken were often rewarded for their time with gifts. In Mary's case – the girl who would become Moll Anthony – that gift was 'the cure'.

Despite established conventions in Irish folklore studies that emphasize the traditions of the west, an exploration of legend traditions in this area of Kildare has proved quite fruitful. A large portion of these traditions are narratives of fairies and their interactions with humans. A vibrant cluster of these stories deals with the character of Moll Anthony. This chapter has provided a context for fairy legend and has situated Moll within that discourse. The next chapter will explore the application of fairy belief, concentrating on narratives of the fairy-woman as healer.

3. Application of fairy belief: folk medicine and fairy doctors

It was said she was in league with the fairies, and they charmed her with cures ... Anyway in her time crowds came to her cabin looking for help and advice for any sickness or misfortune of one kind or another ... Fairy-doctor were the words they called her.[1]

Jack the Cobbler, on Moll Anthony

SUPERNATURAL MEDICINE AND FAIRY GIFTS

In the town of Naas, Co. Kildare, just beyond the bounds of the railway station, lies a field of some importance to the local community. The townspeople remember the field for the flowers that grow there, plants that contain a cure for a sore chest. It is known as the Fairy Flax, for it is said, 'People thought the fairies had something to do with the cure'.[2] As the previous chapter illustrated, the belief in fairies and the supernatural was once widespread throughout Ireland, and continued to exist to a lesser extant well into the 20th century. Even 30 miles from Dublin city, in the area of Co. Kildare surrounding the Hill of Grange, a belief in the fairies persisted at least until the 1930s, when this narrative of the Fairy Flax was collected. This story is exceptional, however, not only for its illustration of active fairy belief, but also because it shows the close connection often drawn in folk culture between the supernatural and issues of sickness and healing – the Fairy Flax is not only a field occupied by the fairies, but it contains a plant with healing properties.

This narrative also provides a neat parallel for the characterization of Moll Anthony. While fairy flax is the name of a plant that grows wild in Ireland (*Linum carthaticum*),[3] this particular field seems to be named for the supernatural healing properties of the plants growing within it. Stories of the field therefore become almost as complicated as those told of Moll Anthony, combining medical knowledge, supernatural belief, and a deep connection to the landscape. All at once, the Fairy Flax is a fairy-touched plant, a cure and a field in the natural world. In much the same way, Moll Anthony is characterized as a fairy-woman, a doctor and an unusual woman of power within her community. These salient aspects of her legend will be examined in this chapter.

As explained in the previous chapter, human interaction with the supernatural is a particular fascination of Irish folk culture, and countless stories are told of those who are taken away for a time to live and learn in the Middle Kingdom. These journeys into another world were not without consequences, however, and those who travelled with the fairies for any length of time rarely emerged from their experience unchanged. In the case of Moll Anthony, her extraordinary powers were popularly attributed to the supernatural, be it the fairies or a more malevolent source. Reidar Christiansen argues that fairy belief developed as a response to unanswered questions about some of life's uncertainties:

> the untimely death of young people, of mysterious epidemics among cattle, of climatic disaster, of both wasting diseases and strokes, of infantile paralysis and of the birth of mongol and otherwise deficient children.[4]

As evidenced by this list, many of these inexplicable areas of Irish life involve mysterious illnesses. In the face of such uncertainty and fear Moll Anthony, a woman gifted with the cure by the fairies, would have been a source of wariness and hope. The stories told of her make it clear that she was different, that she was somewhere between a woman and a fairy. Because of her liminal position, it was thought that she could provide answers to some of those questions, and perhaps even act on behalf of those plagued by the unexplainable.

Among her numerous uncanny abilities, it is her ability to cure that was most well known and which led to her being labelled a fairy-doctor. Of the 30 stories collected for this study, 13 of them deal directly with a cure. Both in published and manuscript form, the stories range in date from 1870 to 1956, covering generations of storytellers, both primary witnesses and secondary reporters. Although the stories of her cures suggest unusual circumstances, it was not unusual in itself for people other than trained medical doctors to treat the sick. According to Logan, in times past medical doctors were largely unavailable in the country, and when they were available they were expensive. For this reason the rich sought out doctors while the rest of the population generally looked to local healers.[5] Local healers were also used for another reason. Before the beginnings of modern medicine in the 17th century, people did not have rational explanations for illness, and so they looked for other sources. Seán Ó Súilleabháin writes:

> It seemed obvious to them that the blame for bodily disabilities could be laid solely on either inimical beings (fairies, spirits, the dead and such) from an invisible outside world, or else on enemies who, by means of the evil eye, tongue or heart, could cause physical harm to those whom they disliked.[6]

These beliefs persisted long after the introduction of modern medicine, and so local healers versed in these beliefs were thought to have the ability to heal diseases that medical doctors without this knowledge could not.

Folk healers like these were generally divided into two categories: those who were born with, or through ritual obtained, a cure for a particular ailment, and those who received or inherited 'the cure', which included the ability to cure any number of illnesses. Within Moll's community, as reported in the Schools' Manuscript Collection, there were at least three healers of the first category actively healing into the 1930s: 'Mrs Brady, caretaker of St Corban's Cemetery, Naas, is able to cure the measles';[7] 'A man named Behan of Ballinrahan Rathangan, cures wasting or fever in delicate children';[8] 'A mixture of herbs to cure "wild fire" is made by Mrs Dawson, Rathangan, Co. Kildare'.[9] Healers that fit into the second category were viewed differently than those in the first, who generally lived as integrated members of the community. Those in the second category, like Moll, were often thought to have obtained their cure from the fairies; although respected, they were also feared. It was these healers that were often known as fairy-doctors.[10]

The difference between fairy-doctors and other folk healers is often difficult to ascertain. The same healer may be believed by some to have obtained the cure from the fairies while others may believe the cure is a gift from God or is some form of witchcraft. It is this mystery surrounding these healers that gave them most of their power. They themselves were not understood and their abilities unexplainable, so they had a great deal of influence over the interpretation of other unexplained phenomenon – in this case, over ideas of sickness and healing. Just who these healers were, and are, is also difficult to ascertain. James Mooney, in his 1887 report on the medical mythology of Ireland, writes: 'The medical professors of this region [Gaeltacht regions in the west] are generally old women, whose stock in trade consists of a few herbs and simple decoctions, a number of prayers and secret formulas to be recited while applying the remedy, and a great deal of mystery.'[11] However, Peter W. Nolan, in his interviews in the 1980s with 'quacks', reports that his informants believe, 'there were more male practitioners than female'.[12] This discrepancy between 19th- and 20th-century healers may in fact be due to the authors' relationship to the subject matter. While Mooney discusses fairy-healers in tradition, and most likely the storytelling tradition, Nolan interviewed active healers. The difference between the archetypes of the stories and the realities of actual practice might provide an explanation.[13] It is of course also possible that the demographics of the practice have themselves changed over time.

Within the storytelling tradition, there are a few famous male examples of fairy-doctors. O'Hanlon describes the character, Paddy the Dash, in his book on Irish folklore. He writes that Paddy obtained his cure from living very close to a rath.[14] Jeremiah Curtin also collected a story about another famous healer, Maurice Griffin the fairy-doctor, who obtained his cure from drinking milk from a cow that had licked up a cloud that had settled on the hill. Curtin writes that after Maurice drank the milk, he could 'foretell right away and cure people.'[15] Along with these more famous characters, the image of an old woman with uncanny abilities who is a source of fear and awe to her community appears again and again. Some of these women are unnamed, but others have become very well known. Thanks to Lady Gregory and her collections of Irish folktales and beliefs, the most famous of the fairy-doctors is a woman named Biddy Early. The stories told about Biddy are remarkably similar to those told about Moll.[16] Moll, Biddy, and women like them, were labelled fairy-doctor, but also fairy-woman, *cailleach luibe* (herb hag) and *bean feasac* (knowing woman), for their extensive knowledge of the plants and charms that were effective in combating both natural and supernatural illnesses.[17] People came from all over Ireland to visit the more well known among them, searching for answers, cures, and advice.

NATURAL AND SUPERNATURAL ILLNESS

The fairy-woman's ability to heal the sick usually extended to both humans and animals, and people came just as often to save calves or a sick mare as they did to help a loved one or a neighbour.[18] Although many people knew folk remedies to cure household injuries and basic sicknesses, when their own cures failed they turned to the fairy-doctors. They had faith in the fairy-doctor's exceptional position as negotiator between the worlds, and believed that this position meant they had special knowledge, as well as special abilities to interfere in cases of natural and supernatural ailments. In Moll's case, of the 13 stories directly related to cures, seven are narratives of the search for human cures, while six are stories of sick animals; also, five stories deal with an illness or circumstance of supernatural cause, while the remaining stories involve natural ailments, or the nature of the illness is not specified.

As evidenced by the breakdown of Moll's cure stories, and the stories of many others, it is clear that although fairy-doctors are often associated with supernatural illnesses, they were also known for treating difficult ailments of more natural origins. Logan in his book, *Making the cure: a look at Irish folk medicine*, details many of the ailments for which folk cures exist.[19] Some of the more frequently treated illnesses include warts, styes, sprains, thrush, skin ailments, headaches, burns, and boils. Most folk cures are for external ailments, although some cures also exist for internal illnesses, such as whooping cough and stomach ailments. Complicated diseases, such as cancers and nervous diseases, were not well understood, and so cures for them are rare.

The information collected from Moll's community in the Schools' Manuscript Collection illustrates the varied ailments that the local folk-medical tradition included. While most of the cures are for similar ailments to the ones listed in Logan's book, there are a few exceptional cures. There are also cures listed for other dangerous illnesses such as consumption and 'wild fire' or 'St Anthony's fire', a dangerous form of necrosis, along with cures for everyday injuries. The collector, Bean Uí Dhubhshláine, describes the most unusual of the ailments treated within this community. She writes: 'One "disease" however, exists here of which I have not heard before. It sounds like "min-iréarac" but nobody I have asked can spell it. The patient rapidly loses weight, energy and appetite.'[20]

With illnesses such as these, fairy-doctors were turned to only after all other attempts at healing had failed. As mentioned before, most people would know at least some of these household remedies, and neighbours with single cures could also heal. When an illness or injury did not respond to these treatments, it was then that Moll Anthony was called upon. Most of the stories about Moll, however, do not name the illness for which she was sought out, instead saying that a child or cow is sick. For this reason, it is difficult to ascertain which natural ailments Moll was asked to cure. However, according to Fitzgerald, Moll was famous for her 'power in curing paralysis, fits, strokes, and other ailments in man and beast'.[21] Although Fitzgerald lists these illnesses as if they are natural illnesses, they are also frequently associated with supernatural influences.

It is these illnesses of supernatural origins for which fairy-doctors were most often sought. After household remedies, and often the attempts of trained medical doctors, had failed to cure an illness or injury, it was often thought that the supernatural played a part in the ailment. For this reason, ordinary attempts at healing were ineffectual, and the special knowledge of a fairy-doctor was required. Some of these supernatural illnesses were the fairy blast, the fairy stroke, and the evil eye. Logan, in his book, *The old gods*, describes these three illnesses in detail. The fairy blast, or the fairy wind, is a whirlwind caused by the passing of the fairy host. The fairies may strike down anything, or anyone, that gets in its way. Logan writes: 'The sufferer who appeared to be in his good health would suddenly fall down and lose consciousness.'[22] Because the sudden decline of an otherwise healthy person could not easily be explained, the fairy wind and the intolerance of the fairies for those who got in their way provided some sort of explanation. Although there are no stories pertaining to the fairy blast among those collected from Moll's community, one of her own cure stories relates its effects on two young girls.[23] The story begins when a young girl comes home from school limping and is questioned by her parents. She then responds that she had left the road to pick cowslips, and had been approached by a beautiful woman near the rath. When the woman asked for the flowers, the girl refused: 'On her refusing to do so she fancied she heard the sound of wings beating the air, and in a moment she was caught in a whirlwind that lifted her off her feet, spun her around, and then dashed her to the ground'.[24] Every remedy was tried and doctors were called, but the girl's legs became weak and crippled. Three years later, the very same thing happened to her little sister while picking primroses near the rath, and she suffered an identical fate.

This story seems to combine the supernatural illnesses of the fairy blast and the fairy stroke, the next of the fairy illnesses discussed by Logan. While the girls were thrown into the air and then dropped on the ground by the fairy wind, they both afterwards complained of sharp pains in their hips, a symptom very similar to that of the fairy stroke. Logan describes the fairy stroke as unexplained and sudden illness, such as an epileptic fit, or severe pain in a long bone caused by osteomyelitis or a tuberculous infection.[25] The latter illnesses present similar symptoms to those experienced by the two girls in the story. Similarly, Mooney writes: 'ulcers, scrofula and running sores were commonly called "fairy strokes", and attributed to fairy influence'.[26] Fairy stroke was also found within Moll's community, as Patricia Meade from Naas lists a cure.[27] Also, humans were not the only ones to be affected by fairy stroke or fairy darts. Joseph Meehan describes the symptoms of an elf-struck cow as follows:

> She is ailing, and has gone back in her milk of course. But if, besides, her hair is standing along her back like a porcupine's quills, if her ears are lifeless and hanging, and her tail when twisted fails to manifest its usual anxiety to right itself, she has most of the symptoms of being 'struck'.[28]

Similarly, in one of Moll Anthony's cure stories she is brought a sick horse that displays symptoms of a fairy-stroke. Statia Costello, a schoolgirl from Naas who contributed this story, writes: 'One valuable horse became paralyzed and he brought it to Moll … It is believed that the fairies paralyzed the horse.'[29] Paralysis is thought to be another symptom of fairy stroke, along with fits and lameness, as evidenced by Statia's assertion that the local people believed the fairies hurt the horse.

The third type of supernatural illness for which fairy-doctors were often sought is the result of the evil eye, or being 'overlooked.' This class of ailments was not caused by the fairies, but instead was caused by the glance of a person in possession of the evil eye, an attribute often thought to be in the possession of women with red hair, along with others.[30] Mooney writes that those in possession of the evil eye, when praising a person, animal, crop, etc., 'intend evil toward the person or thing thus spoken of, and measures are at once taken to prevent it'.[31] Those measures include spitting on the object of praise, and saying 'God bless you'. Oftentimes, the person with the evil eye was asked to come back and perform these rituals in order to undo the harm they had done.

Among the stories of Moll's cures there is also a story of the evil eye.[32] In this case, a farmer had let his sow out near the roadside, and after being out one day, the pig snored all night and would not eat the next day. The man believed 'the poor sow was either "overlooked" or got "a blast".'[33] When he goes to visit Moll, she informs him that his pig was 'overlooked' and it was too late to save her.

The last two stories of Moll's dealings with supernatural illness pertain not to a specific disease, but instead to the switching of fairy changelings for healthy humans. When dealing with changelings in Irish folk culture it is important to remember that people did not believe that their loved ones were sick, but that they had been taken and replaced with sickly, wizened, and often cranky changelings. Therefore, if a person exhibited a sudden change in behaviour or rapid decline in health, such as a wasting sickness, it was often believed that this new unpleasant and unhealthy creature was a changeling. As discussed previously, nearly anyone could be taken and a changeling left in his or her place. In this way, the belief in changelings helped to explain the effects of debilitating diseases such as tuberculosis and nervous disorders, death resulting from childbirth, and high rates of infant mortality due to congenital defects and wasting diseases.[34] In the face of such terrible diseases and illnesses that were not well understood, fairy-doctors were often sought out to try to retrieve loved ones from the fairies and send back the changelings.[35]

There are two stories within the collection used for this study that describe fairy kidnappings.[36] In both instances, the families of the lost children sought out Moll Anthony for help. In the first story, a pretty baby girl is snatched from her cradle after her parents hear 'what they thought was a bee buzzin in the chimbly, an' twas sthrange to hear a bee buzzin in a winter's night.'[37] Although a changeling is not left in its place, this story follows the same pattern as the other story of a fairy kidnapping.[38] In this second story, a young boy remembers that one night, after 'a terrible wind blew, which strange to say, did not blow anywhere only here', he woke up to find his household much changed. He says:

> But the morning after the wind, I saw that both my mother and my father looked very worried, and that the baby seemed very cross, and could not be put to sleep, nor could he the following night but cried continuously with a mournful whine, and I remember when I stole a look at him in his cot, he seemed to be about half Tom's size, and his face looked old and pinched.[39]

This description of the infant is a very characteristic depiction of a changeling – small size, pinched features, and cranky behaviour.

HEALING: PLANT CURES AND CHARMS

As varied as the illnesses for which fairy-doctors, such as Moll Anthony, were sought out were, the treatments and cures that they performed were just as varied. Cures generally consisted of herbal potions, charms, or a combination of the two. Herbal potions or mixtures were often used in households to cure illnesses of natural origins, and many people had knowledge of herbs for both prevention and treatment of illnesses and injuries. In his book, *Irish wild plants*, Niall Mac Coitir lists and describes the plants most often found in Irish folklore and folk medicine.[40] The plants used in folk medicine are too numerous to describe in detail here, but there are patterns in their use and consistencies between Irish communities. Usage of plants depended on availability and knowledge, so variations do occur.[41] The plants used within Moll's community are largely consistent with the lists of plants compiled by Mac Coitir, although more household ingredients such as carrot and garlic were also used. In some instances, the plants were used by themselves in poultices and boiled in milk to affect a cure. There are many examples of this from Moll's community: 'A bunch of mint tied round the wrist is a sure remedy for disorders of the stomach',[42] and 'Vervain boiled cures jaundice'.[43] Some cures are much more complicated, and require multiple plants. An example of this would be the cure for consumption provided by Josie Stafford, who learned about herbs from her grandfather:

> 120 gms Marshmallow root, 240 gms Liquorice Root, 240 gms Linseed, 240 gms Iceland Moss, 120 gms Golden Seal, 120 gms Life Root, 120 gms Pleurisy Root. I am not aware of the processes he out those ingredients through, but it was not very long till the person was cured.[44]

Complex recipes such as this one are rarer in the archive materials than the single plant associations with cures for particular illnesses.

Along with being used to cure natural illnesses, certain plants were also used to combat ailments of supernatural origins. One of these plants is lady's-mantle (Dearna Mhuire; *Alchemilla vulgaris*). Mac Coitir writes of the plant: 'A characteristic of lady's-mantle is that large drops of dew collect in the base of the leaves, and in folk belief this dew possessed magical properties. In Ireland and Scotland lady's-mantle was used to cure people and animals from fairy bewitchment and the "evil eye".'[45] Meehan also lists lady's-mantle as a plant with supernatural connections.[46] The other plant most frequently associated with supernatural illness is foxglove (Lus Mór; *Digitalis purpurea*). Mac Coitir writes of the plant: 'Foxglove contains the powerful drug digitalis, which affects the heart. This made foxglove a mysterious fairy plant, both feared and respected.'[47] As a result of this association with the fairies, as well as the properties of the drug contained within it, foxglove was often given to those suffering from wasting sicknesses – those thought to be changelings or at least under fairy influence. The leaves were given to sick infants to chew, or they were boiled to make tea for ailing adults. Sometimes, infants were submerged in a bath of foxglove-infused water.[48] In Moll's community, one child reported a cure for fairy-stroke using foxglove: 'When children are pining away, they are supposed to be fairy-struck, and the juice of twelve leaves of foxglove may be given.'[49] The foxglove, demanding both fear and respect, in many ways parallels Moll's own image in the eyes of the Irish people she helped.

When creating her own cures, it has been reported by many that Moll did use herbal potions. Jack the Cobbler, in Meda Ryan's book, reports, 'She was in the habit of putting some secret stuff in a bottle … the magic drop'.[50] Unfortunately, part of the power of the cure was the secrecy of its ingredients, and so the herbs that Moll used are unknown. However, it is likely that she used many of the same herbs that were used by other folk-medical practitioners. What is known of her use of herbs was collected by Fitzgerald. He writes: 'Moll Anthony's cure consisted of a liquid concocted from herbs alone, secretly plucked, and sometimes gathered in very distant places'.[51] After learning the cause of her visitor's suffering, she would go off on her own to mix up the herbal potion, and pour it into three porter, or half-pint, bottles.

Not all cures consisted of herbal potions, however. Charms were used nearly as often as medicines made up of plants. Some of these charms consisted of prayers and incantations. One example of this comes from Moll's community, and is listed as a cure for measles:

> 'The child has the measles', said John the Baptist.
> 'The time is short till he is well', said the Son of God.
> 'When?' said John the Baptist.
> 'Sunday morning before sunrise', said the Son of God.
> The foregoing passage to be repeated three times, kneeling at a cross, for three mornings before sunrise. The child will be cured by the following Sunday.[52]

Another very curious example of this, also from Moll's community, is a cure for toothache that consists of a prayer spoken to the Blessed Virgin and the new moon.[53] As well as prayer charms, certain substances were thought to protect against or cure ailments caused by supernatural forces. These include iron, salt, spittle, dung and other substances that could be considered impure. Iron and salt were supposed to be abhorrent to fairies, while substances such as spittle and dung incensed their sense of purity, and so they avoided it. One instance of this type of charm is recorded from Moll's community: 'Wear an iron ring on the fourth finger of the left hand. Rheumatism will never attack you then.'[54] This cure appears to be a remnant of belief in fairy darts, which caused severe pain and swelling in the hands and feet, and was later recognized as rheumatism. Thus, the prevention of injury due to fairy-darts, the repelling of fairies with an iron ring, is now associated with a preventative measure against rheumatism. Also, the mutability of this practice indicates the changing rather than the death of a tradition. A third type of charm involves the use of animals, and usually the passing on of the illness or injury to the animal used in the charm. A cure for mumps from Moll's community provides a good example: 'Rub the sick person against the back of a pig and the disease will pass on to the animal'.[55] Another cure for jaundice also illustrates this type of charm: 'Jaundice is cured by going out under the legs of an ass'.[56]

Among Moll Anthony's cure stories, several illustrate the use of charms to perform cures. The story of the 'overlooked' sow, which was previously mentioned, involves the use of iron to perform a charm. When the farmer comes to Moll for a cure for his sick pig, she informs him that he is too late to save the already sick sow. However, she promises to help him so that he would never lose another pig, and gives him instructions to perform the charm:

> Go home now an' gether up any oul irons ye have about the place an' clane out yer pig house well says she an' put the oul irons in the corner o' the house an' lave them there, for three weeks without stirrin' them, an' from that out I promise ye ye'll never lose a pig again.[57]

While Moll suggests the use of iron to protect the farmer's pigs from the evil eye in this story, in the second story involving a charm she suggests through a third party that a farmer place a goat among his herd of cows to prevent them losing any more calves.[58]

Along with pure herbal potions and charms, folk medical cures often rely on a combination of the two. This is often the case when supernatural abilities are attributed to plants, and their presence in a charm forms the cure. For example, in Moll's community, a cure for styes in the eye involves both prayer ritual and a plant: 'Nine thorns, from a gooseberry bush to be pointed nine times, for nine successive days, to the eye. The Sign of the Cross should be made with the thorns.'[59] Moll Anthony also usually used a combination of charms and herbal medicines, when one considers the instructions she gave to those who came to her as a charm. Fitzgerald suggests this when he says:

> Very minute instructions were given by Moll Anthony to the purchaser, both as to his conduct on the homeward journey, and as to the method of administering the mixture to the patient; any mistake in carrying out either would make the cure ineffective, and a failure in this respect would end in disaster, as Moll Anthony never proscribed a second time for the same patient's ailment.[60]

Some of these instructions included not falling asleep on the way home, not spilling a single drop of the mixture, and making two trips to obtain the bottles, taking two on the first trip and the third bottle on the second trip. It was not always easy to get those bottles home either. Supernatural beings often interfered, causing extreme fatigue and pain in the feet, the second trip home being worse than the first.[61] Once home, the medicine had to be administered in three doses, each increasingly repulsive to the patient. If any of these instructions were not followed, the cure would fail, and the patient was doomed.

As described in the preceding pages, folk medicine was, and is, very closely tied to systems of folk belief, particularly those involving fairies. Moll Anthony received her ability to heal from the fairies, and so she had special power to heal illnesses and injuries caused by the same. Unlike some fairy-doctors, however, Moll also cured sicknesses of more natural origins. Fairy-woman and fairy-doctor were not the only guises that Moll Anthony wore, however; her character is much more complex than these first two layers of tradition reveal. Her connection to the landscape and her social roles within her community, as well as her position within traditions of folk belief and practice, all contribute to her complex character – a powerful woman of many names and faces.

This chapter has examined two aspects central to an understanding of Moll Anthony's legend. Inexplicable illnesses of varying forms were attributed to supernatural causes or to malevolent human actions such as the evil eye. The attribution of supernatural causes to the origins of disease meant that supernatural aid was often sought in healing. Supernatural healing, in turn, involved a combination of charms and herbal remedies. The next chapter will explore further connections between Moll Anthony's legend and power and older mythological narratives embedded in the Kildare landscape.

4. Powerful women and women of power

She used various herbs to effect cures, but it is said that she was in communication with the devil. She often cast charms and spells over those whom she considered her enemies, or over those who injured her in any way either by word or deed. [1]

Kathleen Coffey, on Moll Anthony

WISE-WOMAN AND SOCIAL AUTHORITY

Moll Anthony was known far and wide for her exceptional healing abilities, but she was also influential in her community for other reasons. She was not only a fairy-doctor, who worked with herbs and charms to cure the sick, but also a wise-woman and a respected, if often feared, member of the community. Referring to fairy-doctors and folk healers, Nolan writes: 'As well as they know their own community, so are they themselves known and trusted.'[2] This special relationship meant that Moll and wise-women like her were ideally placed for a role of leadership within their communities. While people outside the tradition often misunderstood Moll's role in the community and the source of her powers, those within the tradition, as a part of the cultural context that supported her role, recognized her as a valuable leader. Like other fairy-doctors and wise-women, both her own supernatural powers and her interaction with the supernatural set her apart from the community: she could not be considered either entirely human or entirely fairy. It was her liminal position that marked her as a source of special knowledge and advice, not only in regard to health and illness, but also in matters involving social justice.

Moll's power within the community was mostly a direct response to the belief that she had been 'away with the fairies', or at least was in communication with them. Her interaction with the supernatural was a source of mystery, and, as Bourke points out, this association would have given her a degree of freedom that, as a woman, she would not normally have been able to attain. Bourke writes: 'A woman had a certain amount to gain, in terms of privacy, prestige, and sanction for subversions of her social role, if she admitted or claimed to have been "away with the fairies".'[3] Because of her association with the fairies, Moll was a source of awe and fear for many, and so she was largely left alone unless her help was needed. She also became well known throughout Ireland, according to the stories, and was able to make a living for herself by collecting payment for her cures. All of these freedoms and privileges were a direct result of her supernatural associations. The assumption by the people that Moll's associations also meant she had special knowledge led to her services being sought for all kinds of social problems.

As a result of this, Moll Anthony can be classified not only as a fairy-doctor but also as a *bean feasa*, or wise-woman. Her position as a wise-woman meant that she acted as a mediator between the worlds, and so could explain the unknown to those who sought her help. According to Nancy Schmitz, the roles of wise-woman and bean leighis, or healer, did not overlap. She writes that the wise-woman's 'contribution was her psychic knowledge of the supernatural world and its happenings, a specific knowledge, limited to cures caused by fairy mischief or similar causes.'[4] She then provides the example of Biddy Early, who did not treat patients who had already seen a doctor, and who would have nothing to do with 'ordinary illnesses or specific ailments'.[5] Ó Crualaoich, however, suggests that wise-women did sometimes perform 'ordinary' medicine, and in fact used herbs to perform cures.[6] This certainly appears to be the case with Moll Anthony, as she is continually associated with herbal remedies, and for curing ordinary as well as supernatural illnesses.

Moll does not, however, fit many other of Ó Crualaoich's descriptions of the *bean feasa*. For one thing, Ó Crualaoich describes the *bean feasa* as usually appearing very old, while very few depictions of Moll describe her this way. It is only in the more romanticized and obviously embellished stories that she is characterized as 'the rale oul Moll Anthony'.[7] Also, Ó Crualaoich says that most *mná feasa* characters are unmarried itinerants, while Moll is very specifically tied down to one place, and is usually thought to have been married.[8] His description of the *bean feasa's* role, however, describes Moll's social role very well:

> Another aspect of the wise-woman's status is that she is regarded as an oracular authority for her community regarding the meaning and significance of experiences they fail to understand – accidents, misfortunes, mysterious illness. Because of this she is regarded with a certain respectful awe mingled with anxiety in respect of her extraordinary and supernatural endowments of knowledge and power.[9]

Lastly, Ó Crualaoich reports that most of the bean feasa legends that he has worked with ascribe supernatural powers to the wise-woman due to her travels with the fairy host. Again, Moll's situation differs from this slightly, as it is not stated in any of the stories used for this study that Moll continually travelled with the fairies. All that is said is that she was thought to be in communication with them. This may imply that she travelled with them, but it may also reflect her comparatively stationary status as opposed to the itinerant lives of the other wise-women Ó Crualaoich studied.[10]

The collection of stories about Moll used for this study illustrates a few of the social problems for which Moll's help was sought. In rural, farming communities, from which most of Moll's patients seem to have come, livelihoods depended on the health of livestock and the production of goods such as milk and butter. Any losses in these areas could spell disaster for farming families. Therefore, when animals went missing or butter failed to form in the churn, Moll was sought out to find the animals and determine the identities of profit thieves. One man, William Byrne, from Co. Wicklow describes his recollections of Moll Anthony and the stories he heard of her as a young man.[11] He says, 'people used to go to her to get their sick animals cured and *their profits back.*'[12] He then also says, 'In another case Moll got back a mare for a man which was gone for two years.'[13] Unfortunately, he does not elaborate how exactly she did this, but he makes it clear that she was sought out for such problems.

By far the most frequent social problem for which Moll's help was sought was the theft of profit, as mentioned by Byrne. Theft of profit usually meant that the ability to make butter had been stolen: no matter how long one worked at the churn, butter would not form. There are three examples of stolen butter profits within the collection of stories used here.[14] The first of the three stories describes a young boy unable to make butter after a neighbouring woman comes to beg 'the seed o' the fire' from them on a May morning.[15] The second story tells of a farmer with six or eight cows producing no butter while his worker, who owned only one cow, brought large quantities of butter to market every week. Along with the farmer in the third story, who suspected his butter was being stolen, the men went to Moll Anthony looking for answers. Despite the different sources of these three stories, the advice she gave to the three men is nearly identical: 'Next time you are churning put the chains of the plough around the churn; put the coulter of the plough in the fire, make it red hot and then plunge it into the churn when the butter should be forming.'[16] In all three stories, once the coulter was plunged in the churn, the profit thief came running to the window or door, screeching in pain, and butter was ever after plentiful in their households.

MOLL ANTHONY AND THE CATHOLIC CLERGY

By mediating in social situations and providing advice so that thieves might be caught and good luck was restored, Moll Anthony played an important role in the community as a leader and as a dispenser of justice. While she was valued by those who believed in her powers and ability to do good, her unusual social role and independence meant that she also made enemies. She was not alone in this regard, as wise-women and folk-healers in the storytelling tradition are often placed in conflict with disbelievers and those who were threatened by their position. Because Moll is connected to the supernatural the figures most often placed in opposition to her, and wise-women like her, were the other class of people associated with the divine – the clergy. Cara Delay goes as far as to say, 'A thorn in the side of the institutionalized church, the wise-woman or healer stood as the priest's main enemy'.[17] Naughton writes of the clergy, 'the powers attributed to many priests and religious to perform miracles are all suggestive of an organization whose members enjoyed a divine or magical authority'.[18] It was this very authority that Moll Anthony challenged, especially as she filled many of the roles usually attributed to the clergy: those of leader, confessor, advisor and healer.[19]

Often, these conflicts arose when a new priest arrived in a parish in which a wise-woman or folk-healer already performed many of the roles intended for the priest. In such cases, the priest often felt his authority threatened by his competitor and did not fully understand the role that she or he played. Also, with the passing of the 19th century, priests came increasingly from middle-class households that did not practice, let alone understand, the folk culture and beliefs of the rural communities in which they served.[20] This left more room for conflict when these two independent and empowered individuals came into contact in these communities. The result of these confrontations is a body of legends that Pádraig Ó Héalaí has termed 'The priest's stricken horse', in which a priest denounces a wise-woman in front of her community, after which his horse falls sick, and he is forced to go to her for help.[21] After agreeing to leave her alone from then on, the horse's health is usually restored by the wise-woman. A prime example of this story type involves Moll Anthony herself.[22]

The story begins with a new parish priest arriving in the town: 'Once a new parish priest came to Allen and soon after his arrival he denounced Moll from the pulpit, on a certain Sunday during Mass.' After this performance, he returned home to find his beautiful horse on death's doorstep. He tried everything to cure the horse, but was eventually convinced by his parishioners to go to Moll Anthony for help. When he arrived at her door, 'she received him rather coldly at first, but in the end she said, "Your horse is cured go home, and in future let me alone, and I will leave you in peace".' Although the story does not explicitly state that Moll herself had caused the horse's illness, her last statement implies that she will do no further damage if he leaves her be, suggesting that she did cause the illness. It was for actions such as these, the purposeful damaging of others or their property, that most often brought Moll's activities and associations into question. Also, it is not suggested that she attended the Mass, and so she heard the priest's denunciation from afar, and caused his horse to be sick, all in the space of time that it took the priest to speak his condemnation and walk home. Her power is affirmed not only by these supernatural acts, but also by the admission of the priest that her power is stronger than his. It was this power, even if used for good, that made her an object of fear and awe and would have her associated with darker forces than the fairies.

Among the powers shared by the priests and wise-women, the ability to heal is of particular interest in the case of Moll Anthony. It was widely believed that priests had the ability to heal if they wished, but that they usually refused to do so. In fact, the church often restricted supernatural healing even when the power to heal came from God. Timothy Corrigan Correll points out that, 'Irish catechisms often included injunctions against superstition and healing in their exegesis of the First Commandment.'[23] The Irish clergy went so far as to prevent their own members from performing cures, even though many of their saints had been exulted for just such practices. One example of this comes from Moll's own community, with the case of the locally canonized Fr Moore. A very holy curate, he used to wander the countryside at night performing cures, until he was silenced by his bishop and moved into a ruined house beside a well to live out the rest of his days. The well continues to be a sight of pilgrimage for those seeking cures to this day.[24]

THE WITCH OF THE RED HILLS

The prohibition against healing such as that of Moll Anthony, and especially Fr Moore, seems strange when the Christian nature of many of these cures is examined. As previously illustrated, many cures and charms were performed with the recitation of prayers. Similarly, water from holy wells was often used to cure various ailments, and pilgrimages to holy wells were frequently performed in order to obtain a cure.[25] Regardless of these connections, healing of a supernatural nature was set in opposition to Christianity by the church, and so was often associated with demonic alliances and evil powers. When paired with accusations of malevolent intentions, the demonic associations of such healing rituals sometimes led to their practitioners being labelled something other than wise-women. The term that was sometimes used for such supernatural women was 'witch'.

The subject of witchcraft is an interesting one in Ireland, for, as Schmitz writes, 'The usual type of European witch was unknown in Celtic tradition, and only existed in the parts of Ireland under Norman influence.'[26] Ó Héalaí also refers to the 'relatively infrequent manifestations of demonic witchcraft in Irish folk tradition'.[27] Although a widespread belief in witches was not part of the native Irish tradition, accusations of witchcraft did occur from time to time, as Schmitz indicates, mostly in areas deeply influenced by international sentiments and the teachings of the institutionalized church. O'Hanlon writes of this: 'In the parts of Ireland settled by the English or Scotch more traces of popular belief in magic practices and in the wizards' or witches' profession remain, than in our purely Celtic districts.'[28] Bob Curran in his book, *A bewitched land: Ireland's witches*, tells the stories of the few prominent witch trials known to have occurred in Ireland.[29] In general, however, there is a distinct lack of witch belief in Ireland, and only with outside influence did people begin to view those with supernatural power as witches.

The figure of the *bean feasa* is a well-known one in Irish tradition. However, those outside of the tradition, who were influenced by imported sentiments and church teachings, regarded her character as very similar to ideas of witches elsewhere. Therefore, as the idea was introduced, the use of the term seems to have increased, and was largely associated with isolated, supernaturally gifted wise-women, even if the idea of making a deal with the devil did not exist in native tradition. In this way, tenants of fairy belief were associated with corresponding aspects of witchcraft belief. As Canon J.A. MacCulloch points out, religious interpretation of fairy belief often produced these results: 'Fairies, elves, brownies, water-sprites, forest and woodland folk, were certainly not angels; therefore they must be demons.'[30] Therefore, if the fairies became demons, than those who associated with them became witches.[31]

In her article on the connections between witches' familiars and fairies in early modern England and Scotland, Emma Wilby suggests some interesting connections between the two sets of beliefs. For example, while in Ireland wise-women were usually visited by groups of fairies, or themselves visited fairy raths, in England and Scotland cunning-women were usually associated with solitary fairies, therefore drawing comparisons with witches' familiars.[32] Of further interest, Wilby hints at the existence of vampirism in fairy-human relationships, although she does not go so far as to label it thus. She relates that both familiars and fairy associates often required a gift of blood from those they helped, or would suck the person's blood if food or milk was not left out for them. She also discusses the fairy practice of taking the essence, or toradh, from milk, corn, or animals, essentially draining it of vitality.[33] This act very closely resembles vampirism, especially as the essence of a thing could also be associated with its soul, which was also taken when a vampire drained a person's blood and they became a vampire themselves. However, there is no direct reference to vampirism in any of the Irish material examined for this study, and the mention of this connection is simply to point out possible links between these three belief systems.

How then is Moll Anthony viewed in light of this material? It appears as if her legend follows a similar pattern to that of Biddy Early.[34] In most cases Moll is linked with the native traditions of the bean feasa and the fairy healer. However, in a few cases she is specifically referred to as a witch. Out of the body of stories used for this study, 30 per cent of the time she is referred to as a 'witch' in some way, while in the other 70 per cent she is referred to as a 'wise-woman', 'fairy-woman', or 'fairy-doctor'. Interestingly, the use of 'witch' was more frequent in Moll's community, as both uses of the term 'witch-doctor' were used in stories from the Schools' Manuscript Collection. In one of those stories, the writer goes further in describing Moll's diabolical activities: 'It is said that she was in communication with the devil. She often cast charms and spells over those whom she considered her enemies, or over those who injured her in any way either by word or deed.'[35] This description is reminiscent of the story of Moll and the priest's horse, and in fact was collected from the same girl. Also, the other instance of the use of the term 'witch-doctor' was from another girl from the same school. Therefore, use of the term 'witch' seems to have been very sporadic, which makes sense considering the lack of a native tradition of witchcraft. Without the tradition of witchcraft in Ireland, the label appears to have had little influence over the treatment of Moll Anthony.

THE WOMAN BENEATH THE TRADITION:
THE HISTORICAL MOLL ANTHONY

Although a supernatural aura is usually attached to Moll Anthony's name, since stories have been told about her the tellers have sworn to the veracity of their narratives as well as to the existence of this extraordinary woman.[36] Despite this insistence on the truth of the stories, which is a common element of storytelling in Ireland in general, attempts at tracking down the historical Moll Anthony have not produced any concrete evidence that she existed. As Ó Crualaoich points out, this lack of historical evidence is something that Moll shares with many other well known wise-women:

> As ever with legend, the lore of the wise-woman presents itself in the guise of history and truth … In particular, these legends portray the wise-woman as real, human females who have lived in communities within human memory, whose houses are still there and whose presence in everyday living is still remembered.[37]

Ó Crualaoich continues this line of argument, pointing out that, after extensive research by many people, even the historical existence of Biddy Early is not entirely certain. This is certainly also true of the stories surrounding the legend of Moll Anthony. Many of the storytellers mention that her house still stands on the Hill of Grange, or that her son built a slate house in the place of Moll's cottage. She is remembered by those whose relatives or friends visited her. The stories do not, however, provide a great deal of detail about Moll herself, particularly in regard to her appearance.

In most of the stories Moll remains a shadowy figure, where a description might have lent her some humanity. Of the 30 stories used for this study, only two provide any information about her appearance. The first story is a romanticized tale of a cripple's love for a beautiful girl, and the boy's inability to recognize that she loves him for himself. Moll Anthony comes along, and in 'a hard, sharp voice', gives the boy advice, all the time mesmerizing him with her 'piercing black eyes'.[38] In this case, the description of Moll's appearance makes her appear supernatural and intimidating, almost the figure of a nightmare, but it fits very well with the overall tone of the story. The second description, on the other hand, depicts Moll as wholly human: 'a fine, bouncing woman, with red hair'.[39] This description might be deemed more likely to be accurate, as the writer was told this by a man who 'actually visited' Moll.[40] It certainly lends support to the idea that Moll was an historical figure.

The most convincing suggestion for the historical identity of Moll Anthony is provided by Fitzgerald in his article, the result of research and collecting within Moll's community. Fitzgerald suggests that Moll Anthony was in fact a woman named Mary Leeson, the daughter of a man named Anthony Dunne. As Mary would have likely been a popular first name in the area, Fitzgerald suggests that based on local custom she might have used her father's Christian name, Anthony, after her own name to distinguish herself from the others. Fitzgerald also suggests that Leeson was the surname of her husband. He writes that, although she is often associated with the Red Hills, her 'sod-wall cabin' was on the east side of the Hill of Grange, facing the Hill of Allen.[41] Mary Leeson lived to be over 80, died around 1878 and was buried in the chapel yard at Milltown.[42]

There are some problems with Fitzgerald's candidate, however. First, most stories place Moll Anthony in the Red Hills and not on the Hill of Grange, which sits to the north-east, although some of the stories from the 1930s, which do not mention the name Leeson, though place Moll Anthony in Allen or on the edge of the Curragh. Of the most importance, however, is O'Hanlon's account, published in 1870, which states that Moll lived near the Red Hills at the 'Chair of Kildare', a name sometimes given to the Hill of Grange.[43] Therefore, Fitzgerald may have been accurate in suggesting that Moll was from the area of Grange. Second, an alternative suggestion for the origin of Moll Anthony's name is given in one account: Anthony is the surname of the family that adopts Mary after she is kidnapped by the fairies, and it becomes her surname when she marries the oldest son of the family. This account also states that Moll lived in Mullaghmast, however, so it is likely that this story was connected to Moll's legend and does not in fact describe her historical person.[44] The third problem with Fitzgerald's account is the dates that he ascribes to Moll (Mary Leeson). If she was into her eighties when she died in 1878, the earliest she could have been born was 1789. However, Ryan reports that Biddy Early heard a story about Moll Anthony when she was a child and repeated it throughout her life.[45] Biddy is thought to have been born in 1798, by which time Mary Leeson would have been at most 11 years old.

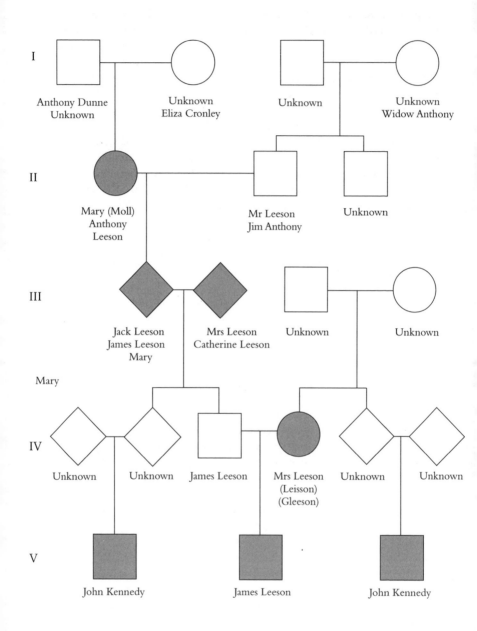

4 Inheritance of the cure in Moll Anthony's family including
variable relations and transference

The story begins by stating, 'Not long ago there was a woman by name Moll Anthony, living near the Red Hills in County Kildare', implying that Moll was no longer alive, let alone a child at the time of the story.[46] These problems do not necessarily mean that Fitzgerald was wrong, however.

Unlike many other wise-women, most stories suggest or clearly state that Moll passed on her 'cure' to members of her family. Piecing together a family tree based on family mentioned in all of the stories it is possible to track the inheritance of 'the cure' through four generations, bringing the existence of healers in the area from the same family up through the 1930s (fig. 4). To begin with, Fitzgerald mentions that at the time of the publication of his article, 1915, 'the cure' is still in the possession of 'her [Moll Anthony's] grandson James Leeson's widow, who still resides in a comfortable slated house on the Hill of Grange.'[47] In support of this finding, there are three references in the Schools' Manuscript Collection from the area that refer to a healer of Moll's quality living around Grange at this time.[48] The first reference states, 'Mrs Leeson of the Red Hills, Rathangan has a cure for everything.'[49] As healers with cures for multiple illnesses were rare, it is likely that this statement refers to the same Mrs Leeson that Fitzgerald reported lived on the hill 20 years earlier. The second reference describes a Mrs Leisson who lived on the Hill of Grange and inherited her cure from an ancestor.[50] According to the collector, this woman died about a year before the story was collected, which would put her death at around 1935. The third reference also describes a healer who lived at Grange and died about two years before the story was collected. This woman was named Mrs Gleeson, but was nicknamed Moll Anthony.[51] It is most likely that all three references describe the same person, with mix-ups in spelling – the same woman mentioned by Fitzgerald.

The importance of this is explained by Fitzgerald, who writes: 'Though Leeson is the family name, yet each generation in possession of "the cure" is popularly still known as "Moll Anthony".'[52] The story of Mrs Gleeson, very probably identical to Mrs Leeson, demonstrates this, as she carried the nickname herself. The reuse of the name could also provide a possible explanation for the problem encountered with Mary Leeson's dates. If her dates seem to be too late for Biddy Early to have heard of her during her childhood, it is possible that the historical Moll Anthony was actually one or two generations removed from the Mary Leeson identified by Fitzgerald. Therefore, Mary Leeson could have been the daughter or granddaughter of Moll, and she carried the name 'Moll Anthony' because she inherited 'the cure' from her. Further possible evidence in support of this argument is the statement in an article in *Ireland's Own*:

Perched on one of the four hills that stand by the western edge of the Curragh was a homestead which in the *eighteenth* century attracted considerable attention from the fact that its owner, a very clever woman, was reported to have uncanny knowledge regarding the compounding of herbs for the cure of various diseases that had baffled the cleverest medical men of the time.[53]

Despite the large amount of evidence that has been collected about Moll, both from her local community and further abroad, it still remains impossible to definitively link her with any one historical figure. It may be said, however, that a contributing factor to the confusion are the many overlapping layers of Moll's character, the bare bones of which are her historical person. She is a fairy-doctor and a wise-woman, but she also exhibits extraordinary powers beyond healing that connect her to another tradition — that of the cailleach, the hag goddess.

MOLL AND THE GODDESS: THE VIRGIN, THE MOTHER, AND THE HAG

No one has ever dared to venture into it, for it is said that anyone who ventures in will not come out. Older people say that an old witch comes out of that cave every year. [54]

Annie Curran, on the Witch's Cave at Grange Hill

One of the many exceptional powers that Moll exhibits in the stories, and which has been reported by many people, is the power of telepathy. Fitzgerald reports that Moll did not treat people who had already seen a doctor, and 'she always had the knowledge, without being told'.[55] He also writes: 'Another marvellous fact was that on the arrival of strangers to consult her, before they had uttered a word, she would acquaint them with who they were, and describe what ailed the patient they sought her advice about.'[56] This assertion is confirmed in a story told about Moll, in which a young boy seeks her advice on catching a profit thief. Upon arriving at her door, the boy is frightened when Moll tells him she knows why he is there.[57]

Moll also seems to have been fairly omniscient, able to know what was going on far away and to hear conversations from a distance. In one instance, a man comes to her because the 'luck' has been taken from his family. Without visiting the property, Moll is able to tell him that his house was built on a fairy path, and that he must fill in the doors and break out a new one to appease the fairies.[58] In another example, a man on his way to visit Moll curses her when his carriage goes into a ditch. When he finally makes it to her door, she says, 'Indeed, Mr. J__, you needn't have cursed Moll Anthony on your way here.'[59] There have also been some suggestions that Moll was capable of foretelling the future. In his less-than-flattering description of Moll, O'Hanlon writes: 'Her reputation as a possessor of supernatural knowledge and divination drew crowds of distant visitants to her daily.'[60] One story supports the idea that Moll was capable of divination. When a man comes to Moll because one of his pigs is sick, she tells him that it is too late to save the pig that is already sick. However, she tells him that if he follows his instructions exactly, that he will never lose another pig. The teller reports that in fact the man did have good luck with his pigs ever after.[61]

It is supernatural powers such as these, combined with other factors, which make an equation of Moll Anthony with other autonomous female deities possible. Many of the unusual qualities of Moll's character are also definitive aspects of one such class of deities, the cailleach or hag. Ó Crualaoich has written a definitive book on the archetype of the cailleach in Irish folktales and the significance of the hag goddess within Irish cultural tradition.[62] One of the aspects of the hag that he highlights is her autonomous personality, her non-sovereignty queen characteristics.[63] He categorizes them under four headings using the Cailleach Bhéarra as a case study.[64] All four of the categories apply to Moll Anthony as well, at least to some degree.

For one, the cailleach is supposed to have had almost superhuman energy, an attribute that Moll demonstrates by travelling great distances to gather herbs for her medicines. Secondly, the cailleach is supposed to have been extremely long-lived or in fact immortal. Moll also seems to fit this description. If the stories are to be believed, Moll has been attributed by various sources with living anywhere from the late 1700s into the early 1900s, stretching her life span far over a century. Another aspect of the physical eternity of the cailleach, as illustrated by Daragh Smyth, is the regenerative power of the hag. She is continually transitioning from hag to virgin and back again, reflecting the changes of seasons and the renewal of the land.[65] It could also be said that Moll Anthony has undergone similar transitions, in that she has been symbolically reborn in successive generations, as her name has been passed down along with the cure. Of further significance, Moll's revival from the dead mirrors the rebirth of the virgin from the hag.

The third aspect of the Cailleach, which Moll exhibits to some degree, is her association with the creation and domination of the landscape. Although she is not attributed with the creation of Ireland or large land areas like the Cailleach, she has influenced and shaped the local landscape. Her name has been associated with Kildare, the Red Hills, and the Hill of Grange, so that this place has become the land of Moll, and her legend is anchored there. Her house still stands on the Hill of Grange, marking her place. But she also lives in the landscape in the form of an unusual feature at the top of the hill – the cave that bears the name of a witch.

The final aspect of the Cailleach Bhéarra identified by Ó Crualaoich is her conflict with and displacement by Christianity. Moll's conflict with the Catholic Church has already been highlighted. Her confrontation with a new parish priest, in the tradition of 'the priest's stricken horse', illustrates her relationship with the church, but also her refusal to be displaced, and the failure of the priest to displace her. While this story shows a particular resilience to the transformative powers of a unified, institutionalized church, she was not unaffected by religious change. As time passed, she was called not only fairy-woman, but also witch, and her associations with the fairies were considered dealings with demons. This trend of transition influenced by the church connects her to another important goddess who became a saint and is coincidentally anchored to the landscape not far from Moll's home. Brigit is perhaps the greatest example of the transformation of a pre-Christian goddess into a Christian saint. Smyth describes Brigit as a goddess of healing and fertility, 'a female sage and wise-woman'.[66] The cult of Brigit, both pre-Christian and Christian, was a powerful representation of female autonomy, one deeply connected to the land, the changing of the seasons, and the passage of time.[67] Brigit was reborn with her transformation from goddess to Christian saint, just as the hag is reborn into the virgin. As a saint, Brigit was described as the Mary of the Irish, a position that perhaps reflects her previous incarnation as a mother goddess.[68] In this way, both the cailleach and Brigit represent a renewal or a reconfiguring of an even older tradition of female power – that of the mother goddess.

Marie-Louise Sjoestedt, in her study of Celtic gods and heroes, describes the classification of Irish gods and goddesses. She writes that while gods tended to be tribal and more widely recognized, Irish goddesses were more local and tied down to particular areas. Also of interest, she notes that goddesses tended to be closely connected to the landscape, much more so than the gods. Reflecting this, there is much more information about the goddesses in the Dindshenchas and much more on the gods in the histories.[69] She also writes:

> We must dismiss the notion of one deity who is titular, as it were, of a particular function, in favour of the notion of diverse realizations of a single religious idea, groups of deities, probably local – at least in origin – who are not identical but equivalent, having evolved among different peoples, perhaps at different times, from the same generative impulse.[70]

For this reason, many of the goddesses of Ireland share responsibility for health and hearth, fertility and sexuality, each serving different local areas. Sjoestedt divides them into mother goddesses and goddesses associated with war and battle, but notes that there are overlaps between the two groups, such as Queen Maeve, who shows characteristics of both.[71]

There are many mother goddesses in Irish mythology and tradition, mainly because of their highly localized associations. As explained by Sjoestedt, these local goddesses all performed similar functions, as opposed to the Greco-Roman model of particular functions for each god and goddess.[72] For this reason, many of the local goddesses were equated with each other, and so one goddess was often thought to have many names and guises. Also, as new groups moved into areas, bringing their gods and goddesses with them, old and new were sometimes combined, further complicating the understanding of the Irish pantheon. These complications, however, sometimes provide some insight into the connections between mythologies and traditions.

A vibrant example of this blending and overlapping of goddess traditions exists within the character of Moll Anthony. As previously illustrated, Moll is connected to traditions of the cailleach and the goddess Brigit, who in turn are both connected to earlier traditions of mother goddesses. However, Moll Anthony herself is also closely associated with another mother goddess figure – the white cow witch that emerges from the cave at the top of the Hill of Grange once every seven years. Mother goddesses have been associated with cows long before the tradition came to Ireland. Hilda Ellis Davidson has described similar traditions in Ancient Egypt, Mesopotamia and India, as well as through the Nordic and Celtic worlds.[73] Even Brigit, both the goddess and the saint, is often associated with white cows. St Brigid is said to have been the illegitimate daughter of a bondmaid impregnated by her master. She was born as her mother crossed a threshold carrying a pan of milk, as Davidson writes, 'symbolizing the liminal position of Brigid between the human and supernatural worlds'.[74] The baby Brigid was bathed in milk and fed with the milk of a white, red-eared cow. Patricia Monaghan also points out that she is, 'often depicted leading a cow'.[75] Of further interest, the white cow with red ears is also associated with the Cailleach Bhéarra, who owned such a cow, and another goddess, the Mórrígan, who claimed to be able to take that shape.[76]

Of importance here, however is the mother goddess Bouvinda, a continental Celtic goddess. Thomas O'Rahilly writes of her: 'The goddess, in addition to being white or bright (*vinda), was often regarded as possessing bovine shape'.[77] Also of importance, Ptolemy in his geography of Ireland lists Bouvinda as the name of the river that is known today as the Boyne. When Bouvinda came to Ireland, however, her name changed and she became Bóand, wife of Neachtain (also Nuadu or Elcmar), the personification of the river. The legend of Bóand becoming the river is an interesting one. Nearby her husband's home at Brug na Bóinne was a well of knowledge, into which only her husband and his servants could gaze. Wanting knowledge for herself, Bóand dared to look into the well. Immediately, the water rose up, destroying one eye, one hand, and one foot and chasing her into the sea.[78] In this guise, Bóand wound about the eastern plains giving life to the land.

Monaghan writes, however, that Bóand is the combination of the continental river goddess and a native cow goddess, Bó Fhionn.[79] She writes: 'One primeval May morning, the radiant Bó Finne and her sisters, red Bó Rua and black Bó Dubh, rose from the sea. Each headed off in a different direction: red to the north, black to the south, Bó Finne to the centre, there to bear the twin calves from whom all Ireland's cattle descend.'[80] The Celtic goddesses of abundance were often connected to rivers, as they provided for the land by giving life. As the Irish depicted the cow goddess as also wandering through the countryside giving life through its milk, the connection was forged between the two, and Bóand was born.[81] It is this many-layered mother, the white cow goddess, whose memory haunts the cave on the Hill of Grange, and whose traditions have been associated with Moll, the 'witch' on the hill. Sjoestedt writes: 'we shall find at every point of the epic tradition similar figures of mothers and teachers, no longer gods but heroes.'[82] Moll Anthony represents one step further along this road – the transition from god to hero to human.

The traditions of wise-women and, to some degree, witchcraft can be shown to be interwoven with the previously discussed legend traditions of fairy-women and healers. Moll's connections to earlier mythological narratives anchored in the nearby landscape were also explored with discussions of the cailleach and mother-goddesses. Significantly, Moll's transition does not necessarily indicate a diminishing: she is human, but she has taken on the attributes of many of her female forbears (the wise-woman, the hag, the mother goddess) and in her stories her power is not diminished at all. She is autonomous: a source of fear, awe, and respect. She is the mother goddess who became the hag, who was reborn as the wise-woman, who lived as a healer. She is like the cave that sits on top of the very hill where she made her home: the home of a zoomorphic mother goddess that was labelled a fairy mound, and is now just a curious feature in the landscape with an interesting name. But the stories remember, even if the people do not, that the calf in the cave is a goddess, and the woman on the hill was more than she appeared.

5. Conclusion: re-evaluating the traditions of the East

The legend and character of Moll Anthony is a complex interweaving of many traditions. This study has provided a look at the wider cultural context in which her character was, and continues to be, forged. First, her position within tradition and popular discourse is influenced by concepts of folk belief, particularly in regard to fairy belief. Her association with supernatural beings such as fairies placed her in a liminal position in which she was gifted with special powers. Second, those special powers included the ability to heal where all other attempts had failed. Moll is therefore connected to traditions of folk medicine and fairy-doctors as well as those of fairy-women. Finally, traditions of supernatural females and their human manifestations also contributed to the formation of Moll's character. The result of this amalgamation of legend traditions is that Moll combines legends of cailleachs, witches, and goddesses with traditions of folk medicine and fairy belief within her human character.

Although it was previously suggested that the character of Moll Anthony was built on the bare bones of an historical figure, one could argue that in fact Moll was created in the opposite direction. Instead of humanity forming her skeleton, it may be more apt to say that her core, her essence, is more divine – that a goddess forms her innermost layer. It could then be said that over time the goddess's glamour was dimmed by changing perceptions of the supernatural. Instead of remaining ageless, she took on the mantle of the hag, existing in a cyclical aging pattern of hag to virgin and back again. As the influence of the goddess grew weaker, she stepped closer to the mortal world, persisting in the liminal position of wise-woman. In this guise she remained important to the people, but was closer to becoming one of them. She moved into the human community entirely when she became a fairy-doctor, a healer and integral part of rural life. As Mary Leeson, or another woman of her kind, the goddess became fully human. However, the layers beneath her mortal form remain within her character: the *bean feasa*, the cailleach, Bó Fhionn and Bouvinda all persist within her form.

The persistence of these traditions within Moll, a character anchored in the mythical landscape inside the Pale, suggests that modernity does not necessitate the death of tradition. Though the faces of many of the traditions have changed, as evidenced by the many-layered qualities of Moll, the core of these traditions remains largely intact. It has been argued that Anglicization, language change, urbanization and industrialization have eroded Irish traditions almost to the point of death; that tradition cannot survive in the face of so much change. However, this may not hold as true as many have feared. The legend of Moll Anthony has proved a rich deposit of overlapping traditions, and yet many of the stories about her were collected in industrialized, urban towns from English-speaking people. As the center of these modernizing processes, the legend traditions of the east of the country continue to be undervalued. However, the case of Moll Anthony suggests that these unexpected places and forgotten sources within the east may in fact prove as rich in tradition as the west.

As Ireland has moved into the modern world, the tendency of tourists and scholars alike to speed through the east to find the 'real' Ireland of the past has become commonplace. Having thoroughly examined the many layers of tradition anchored at the Hill of Grange in the figure of Moll Anthony, it seems strange that this should be true. When the surrounding landscape is considered, the lack of attention to this area seems inexplicable. Within Co. Kildare alone exists the church and fire temple of Brigid, Irish saint and mother goddess; the Hill of Allen, home of the great Irish hero, Fionn mac Cumhaill; and the Sídhe of Neachtain, source of the Boyne and well of knowledge connected to the legends of Bóand and Fionn. When all of Leinster is considered, the historical, mythical, and cultural significance of this landscape is undeniable. Some sites, such as Tara and Newgrange have received an extensive amount of protection, attention and scholarly notice. However, isolating these sites of importance within the larger landscape does not do them justice. Ignoring the surrounding landscape is comparable to recognizing the healer in Moll while failing to understand her greater cultural significance: the surface may be recognized, but the core is not understood.

It is therefore important that the landscape be considered and engaged with as a whole. Acknowledging the importance of grand monuments is not enough. By isolating them, they are stripped of their larger context and significance. Roads are built through sacred landscapes and quarries are dug on holy mountains, demonstrating this failure to understand the landscape as a totality. If the landscape as a whole is not considered, if the places in between the landmarks are ignored as they have been in the east, then deposits of rich cultural traditions such as Moll Anthony *will* remain hidden from the larger population. Engaging with the landscape in this way has historically been a defining characteristic of Irish identity. As Sir William Wilde writes: 'If ever there was a nation that clung to the soil, and earned patriotism by the love of the very ground they walk on, it is (or we may now write was) the Irish peasantry.'[1] As Wilde feared, this engagement with the land has declined, and so many of these traditions are overlooked. In order to rediscover these traditions it may be necessary to re-examine the way in which land is inhabited. Passive existence on the surface is not enough. It is active engagement with the land by inhabiting the landscape alongside history and myth that will open the door to further discovery. The traditions are there – perhaps hidden beneath a mask of modernity, but they persist. One only has to look.

Appendix: the stories

A

The Witch's cave is in the townland of Puncher's Grange, Barony of Connell and Parish of Feigh Cullen. It is said that a white calf comes out of the cave every seven years and if you see that calf and catch hold of his tail when he comes out you will have to go into the cave. It is surrounded by rocks and furze bushes; and has an entrance hole. No one has ever gone down because the entrance hole is very narrow. The owner of the land never interferes with the cave in any way.[1]

B

On the top of Grange Hill, Barony of Connell, Parish of Feighcullen, there is a cave called the 'Witch's Cave'. It is of a round shape with rocks all around it. No one has ever dared to venture into it, for it is said that anyone who ventures in will not come out. Older people say that an old witch comes out of that cave every year. The owner of the land never interfered with it.[2]

C

The Witch's Cave is situated in the townland of Grange, Parish of Allen, and Barony of Connell. It is a vast square cave under a rock with a small hole for an entrance. It is said that an object in the form of a white calf comes out of it every seventh year and if anyone catches him they will have to go in with him. People have often heard the sound of music in it.[3]

D

A man of the name Christy Hickey, who lived and died close to the Moat of Ardscull, on one occasion related to me a curious tale in connexion with Moll Anthony's girlhood; but, as is often the case, he shifted the scene of the story to his own neighbourhood, and, according to his version, Anthony was a surname. According to Hickey, the Widow Anthony lived with her two sons on a small holding at Mullaghmast, and one day she sent her sons to look after some sheep on a field she had taken from a neighbour. After proceeding some way along the road they met a funeral, consisting of four strange men carrying a coffin on a 'bearer'. According to the custom of the country they turned and followed the funeral, and then took a turn in assisting in carrying the coffin. On reaching their mother's gate, they rested the 'bearer' on the road, and, wishing the strangers a God-speed, they made for their house. On seeing them the Widow Anthony expressed her surprise on their getting back so soon, and so they explained the cause, and said: 'With the help of God' they would start again for the sheep. To their astonishment on reaching the road they found the coffin where they had laid it down, and the strangers were nowhere to be seen. Then, acting on their mother's advice, they brought the coffin to the house. The Widow Anthony, noticing that the lid was not screwed down, told them to raise it, and inside they saw 'a grand slip of a gerrel' lying as if she was asleep; the colour was in her cheeks, and warmth in her body. They raised her up, and presently consciousness returned to her. From that day for nine years she lived with them, under the name of Mary, and did the household work. Good-luck and prosperity seemed to have entered the house with her, as the farm throve, though up till then the Widow Anthony had been hard sent to make up the rent. One day, at the end of the nine years, the Widow Anthony said to her elder son: 'Jim,' says she, 'it would be no harm in life if ye put the comedher on the gerrel if she'd fancy ye.' 'Begorra,' replied Jim, 'I was thinking that same meself, as good-luck is better nor any fortune, so it is'. In the end the two were married, and by the time that three children were crawling about the house, Jim said that he would have to go to the Fair in Castledermot to buy a filly. 'I have never asked the like afore, Jim', said Mary, 'But I'm wishful to go wid ye'. 'Come, and welcome, Mary aroon', said Jim; 'shure me mother will mind the childher'. So off they started in the ass-cart, and arrived at the fair. Seeing a suitable filly in charge of a young fellow, Jim bid up to within £5 of the price asked for it, and was referred to the owner, who was in the town with his wife. When they met, Jim and his wife invited the couple to a public house to settle the deal. Noticing that the old man was staring hard at his wife after the bargain was clinched, Jim asked: 'What the blazes are ye looking in that unmannerly way at me woman for?' 'Well, now' said the old man, 'If I wasn't as certain as I have the price of the filly in me breeches pocket, I'd take me oath that that was a daughter – the Lord have merct on her! – that I buried some years ago'. 'Can ye give me the day and the date?' says Jim. 'If I can't,' says he, 'Herself can', and he called his wife over. 'It was the 3rd of May thirteen years ago' says she. 'Bedad that's mighty queer' said Jim; 'shure that's the very day I first laid me eye on me woman'. Addressing Mary, the old woman said, 'Come to the parlour wid me, alanna' says she, 'and I'll soon know if Himself is right'. 'Arrah, mother' said Mary, 'don't trouble to see me stripped, shure I'll not deny that the raspberry mark is on me shoulder'. 'Glory be to God, it's true' said the old woman. 'And that's the way Moll Anthony came to Mullaghmast', finished up Christy Hickey.[4]

E

There was one story which Biddy was to recall and retell many times during her life. One night a few of the neighbours gathered around the hearth, some smoking clay pipes and casting the odd spit into the glowing fire which licked the black chimney. Only the dull light of a candle broke their shadows as it flickered upon the wooden table beneath the little window at the side of the cabin.

Biddy curled herself in a corner away from the grown-ups as she knew from experience that she should not pretend to understand, nor should she ask questions of the elders. Her mother sat on the hob, while her father sat on the wooden block at the other side of the glowing fire.

'Jack, the Cobler' pushed back his cap over his greying hair, and began to tell his tale:

Not long ago there was a woman by name Moll Anthony, living near the Red Hills in County Kildare. It was said she was in league with the fairies, and they charmed her with cures. This is the truth I'm telling ye, for she has a son abroad there today, by name Jack. He's a class of a cow-doctor. Anyway in her time crowds came to her cabin looking for help and advice for any sickness or misfortune of one kind or another. 'Pon my soul, that's the kind of thing she did. Fairy-doctor were the words they called her. She was in the habit of putting some secret stuff in a bottle and told the person who was sick or came to her, 'Don't fall asleep on the way home.'

Begor anyway there was one young woman who had travelled from a neighbouring county to consult this Moll Anthony woman. A relative of hers was very ill. Moll gave her the magic drop in the bottle and said, 'Keep your eyes open on the way home.'

Anam 'on diabhal, after she had walked a good part of the journey, didn't she get woeful tired. Down she sat by the side of a ditch to take her ease a bit, but twasn't long until the sleep overcame her. Then she had this almighty dream. A wrinkled old hag, her teeth gone, with a beak nose and a fierce scowl came towards her as if to clutch her in her long skinny arms. The young woman gave an almighty roar of terror, jumped on her feet and as she did so, the magic bottle fell to the ground, and was broken in little pieces on the stones.

Tis said that the hideous hag of her dream was a spirit from the other world with whom Moll Anthony was said to be in league. Anyway to finish the story, when the young woman got home, she found her sick relative dead in the bed.[5]

F

Fairy Flax- that is the name of a field on Friary Road. Flax – or some kind of flower – grows there and it contains a cure for a sore chest. People thought that the fairies had something to do with the cure and so the field is now called the 'Fairy Flax'.[6]

G

The Fairy Flax is a tract of waste ground in the immediate vicinity of the Naas railway station. On this land there are two trees situated about four or five yards apart. There is a story circulated around the district that every night at 12 o'clock, particularly in the winter, a headless man is seen riding a white horse between these two trees.[7]

H

A schoolgirl from the neighbourhood came home limping. Questioned by her parents as to the cause she told the following strange story.

She had, she said, left her companions and entered a field off the road to pick cowslips. Coming near and old rath she saw a beautiful lady who spoke to her, saying: 'Would you mind giving me those lovely flowers, little girl?'

On her refusing to do so she fancied she heard the sound of wings beating the air, and in a moment she was caught in a whirlwind that lifted her off her feet, spun her around, and then dashed her to the ground. She complained of a severe pain in her hip. A doctor was called in, and every remedy tried, but the leg became feeble and more crippled day by day.

Three years later her younger sister went with other children to pick primroses in the vicinity of the aforementioned rath. She was so intent in the picking of the flowers that she did not miss the other children leaving the field. She hurried after them, but on passing the rath she was surprised to see a youth and a girl most majestically attired in velvet, sitting on its mossy side.

'Little girl' said the youth 'would you mind giving this young lady those nice primroses?'

'Deed an' I won't' the little girl answered sharply: 'I've spent the better part of an hour picking them.'

A couple of seconds afterwards she heard sounds as if wings were beating the air, then, with a jerk she was lifted up, spun around, and then dashed to the ground.

Home she went crying and limping just as her sister three years before.

Things remained like this until an uncle came on a visit, and, having heard the story of their misfortune, he determined to pay a visit to the wise woman of Kildare.

He was up brave and early the following morning, and made straight for the old woman's cottage.

At the door she met him with: 'So you've come at last John Daly – come at the eleventh hour to crave a boon that others should have craved many years ago.'

The uncle of the girls was very much surprised to hear his name spoken by a woman who he never saw before; he sensed a feeling a feeling of awe that was uncommon to him.

'Yes, ma'am' he answered.

'Well,' she said in a low voice, 'for one of these girls there is a hope, provided you will be able to stand the test I will have to lay on you.'

'I will do my best, ma'am. What more can mortal do?'

'Spoken like a brave man, John Daly. And a brave man you have ever been –

but it will require all that determination you inherited from your parents to carry out the task allotted to you.'

'You will abide with me awhile until this brew which is on the fire is finished', she continued. 'When it is ready I will bottle some of the mixture, and then with my blessing you may start on your homeward way. Remember that on your homeward journey the spirit of wind and water, of light and dark shall battle for and against you, for once you leave the shelter of my cottage until you enter the home of the crippled girls, your patience and courage will be tested, but not beyond the limit of human endurance. The test is a severe one, but the results will repay you a hundredfold.'

'Now' she added, 'take this bottle in your hand, and from the time you leave this house till you enter the girls' home, on your peril do not leave it on the ground. If you are so silly as to do so – well, you will pay the price, for misfortune will dog your footsteps all through your life.'

Many a time the girls' uncle told the story of that dread homeward journey, during which his patience and courage were put to the severest test. How invisible hands pinched and clutched at him. How voices, startling, hollow, or pitched in the highest key, bellowed and shrilled around him until his nerves were so shattered that on several occasions he almost dropped the bottle.

Not alone did the uncanny voices annoy him, but at various places on the moor he was tormented by most intense itching of his feet that almost set him distracted.

Yet, in spite of all, he carried the bottle to its destination without a hitch, and had, in the due course of time, the satisfaction of seeing the younger sister grow stronger day by day.

But the liquid, as the old woman had said, brought no relief to the other girl.[8]

I

Moll. Anthony was a witch doctor, who lived on the red hills of Kildare. It was believed that she cured horses and cows of certain diseases. Once a man, named Mr O'Neill had race horses on the hill. One valuable horse became paralyzed and he brought it to Moll. Anthony in order to obtain its cure. She said that he was to give the horse the herb that she would give him. She also said that she would know whether he would give the animal the herb, or not. If he delayed to give it until a certain time it would not take effect. The man forgot about the herb, until two minutes after the time appointed. The horse therefore was not cured. It is believed that the fairies paralyzed the horse.[9]

J

Wan time, long ago, a man, be the name of Lar Casey, had a sow. She was as fine a pig as you could lay your eyes on. but he used to let her out by the roadside to run about an ate a bit o' grass for herself. An befor, someone 'overlooked' her like. She came in, this night, an lay down in the house, an began to snore like, an the next morning she refused altogether to ate a bit. Befor after a day or two, Lar said that he'd go to Moll Anthony to the Red Hills in Kildare, for the poor sow was either 'overlooked' or got 'a blast'. So, he riz early mid-mornin an wint off to the Red Hills.

When he crossed the 'thrassel' Moll was sitting at the fire.

I know yer business, me man, says she, an yer late. 'Tis yer pig is sick, says she. 'Tis ma'am, says Lar: can ye do anything for her. Yer a day late, honest man, says she, for yer pig was 'overlooked' says she. Yer pig'll die to-morra but I'll settle it for ye, that from this out, you'll have good luck in yer pigs, says she.

Go home now an gether up any oul irons ye have about the place an' clane out yer pig house well says she an' put the oul irons in the corner o' the house an lave them there, for three weeks without stirrin them, an' from that out I promise ye ye'll never lose a pig again.

Lar came home an' the sow died the next morning so he done as Moll told him an' he had the best of good luck ever after.[10]

K

They was a man an' woman livin in Cooleyhorgan wan time, an' they had wan child, a little girl.

This night they were sittin' at the fire an' the child was in the cradle asleep. After some time, they heered what they thought was a bee buzzin in the chimbly, an' twas sthrange to hear a bee buzzin in a winter's night.

Befor whin they wint to get ready for bed, the woman wint over to the cradle to take up the child, an wasn't it gone out o' the cradle. The poor father and mother run to the neighbour's houses roarin' and' bawlin' an' they could hear tell in no tale, or trace, o' the child.

So the nixt morning at the break o' the day, the poor man set out to Moll Anthony. When he wint into the house an' tould his story, Moll seez to him. 'How far is the rath from your house' sez she. Only a couple o' hindred yards from the dure sez he.

Well sez she, go to the Rath to-night at the midnight hour an' you'll see the Hunt comin' out says she, an' the first lady that ye'll see ridin a white horse sez she, that's yr child, an' if ye're able to pull her off in the horse sez she, you'll have yer child again.

So befor, the man wint to the Rath, an' to the minnit o' twelve o' clock out comes all the gintlemen an' ladies ridin the horses an' right in the middle was the lady on the white horse. Befor, he med a grab at her an' had her in his arms in no time. She was just like a mushroom in his arms, but he ran so fast, he never looked at her, till he ran in, in the dure, an there sure enough was his own child safe and sound again.[11]

L

You may have heard of my brother, your Uncle Tom (said my father). He went to America as a boy, after your Uncle Peter was transported there as a Fenian.

Tom was a baby, and I was a schoolboy at the time of this happening. One night a terrible wind blew, which strange to say, did not blow anywhere only here. (My father pointed to a lighter-coloured rafter supporting our smoke-blackened thatch.) It cracked the old rafter that was there and later I helped my father to fix up that new one.

But the morning after the wind, I saw that both my mother and my father looked very worried, and that the baby seemed very cross, and could not be put to sleep, nor could he the following night but cried continuously with a mournful whine, and I remember when I stole a look at him in his cot, he seemed to be about half Tom's size, and his face looked old and pinched.

The second day after the wind, I heard mother say to father:

'John, you must go in God's name' and father answered that he would go in the morning.

Strangely Quiet

I did not see him anymore before he went as he was gone before I woke in the morning, and he was not back the following night before I went to sleep, but some time in the middle of the night I woke with a feeling something was wrong, and sure enough there was a wind howling around the house which frightened me, even when it ceased fairly sudden, eventually I slept, and when I woke in the morning, I noticed the house strangely quiet, and I went off to school wondering at the more cheerful appearance of mother and father.

Years afterwards I heard the whole story, and just tell it as I heard it.

It appears that mother and father suspected that the whining wisp of a thing in the cot, the morning after the first wind, was a changeling left by the 'Good People' when they took Tom away during the height of the wind.

To Moll Anthony

They decided that father go to the Red Hills of Kildare where the Fairy woman,

known as Moll Anthony resided, which
father did, and returned late that night
with three bottles of water, which he
sprinkled, according to instructions,
around the house at midnight. Shortly
afterwards the wind arose that woke me
that night, and next morning there was
the old Tom, if I can call him so, anyhow
he was the same robust baby we had
before the first wind, but he almost slept
continuously for days afterwards.[12]

M

A well-to-do farmer in South Kildare had
a large herd of milch cows which were
suffering from the disease now known as
contagious abortion, but which in these
days was called 'dropping calf'. This man
was very hospitable and always kept a bed
in the barn for poor people who had no
homes. One evening a 'travelling woman'
called, and, as usual, was given her supper
by the fireside in the kitchen. The farmer
was complaining of the great hardship he
was suffering through the loss of so many
calves and so much milk. The woman
suggested that he should go to Moll
Anthony for advice, but he said he
couldn't do that, as the Catholic Church
was opposed to such practices as being
superstitious. The woman went away next
morning but returned in about a month's
time, and asked if there had been any
more losses. On being told that there
were, she informed the man that if he
would send up to the Glen of Imaal to a
certain person he would get a young
puckawn goat, and that if he would let
the goat run with the cows there would
be no more losses. The farmer sent his son
(from whose son I have heard this story)
to the Glen of Imaal; he found the house
indicated by the woman and found also
that there was a young puckawn for sale
in the place. He bought the young goat,
and set it free amongst the herd of cows.
About twelve months afterwards the 'poor
woman' came again to the farmer's
house. She inquired about the cows and
was told there were no more losses since
her advice had been taken. She said the

advice was not hers, that when she found
the farmer was unwilling to consult Moll
Anthony she went to the Red Hills
herself, and that the advice he had acted
on was that given by Moll Anthony when
the circumstances of the case were made
known to her.[13]

N

'Twas in a May mornin' a good many
years ago now, an' me mother (God rest
her soul) was an early riser.

Get up Billy, says she to me, this
mornin'. Till we make the churnin. So up
I gets, an' down wid me to the well for a
can o' spring wather. So as to have it to
wash the butter, like. Goin down the road
I met an oul damsel an' she facin for our
house like. Marra Billy says she to me,
Marra an good luck says I, for I didn't
care much for the same damsel an' I
couldn't make out what had her out so
early an' she havin nothing to do, like.
Befor, whin I come back wid the wather,
me mother says to me, Bills, says she, put
on the kittle till we get a sup o' tay.

I knew be her she was knocked about
like so I says to her, 'Are ye goin to get
the tay afore we makes the churnin'.

Yis I am says she, for I', not the same
in meself since that wan came in, lookin
for the seed o' the fire, but I didn't give
it to her though. So, I didn't, says she.
Arrah, musha mother says I. Thims only
pisherogues, come on an' drink the tay, for
be this time, the kittle was bilin.

So we dhrank the tay an' started into
the churnin: meself was a thundherin
hand at the dash. So I tell you. I wasn't
long risin steam.

But befor, if I did, there was no sign o'
the butther. Me mother came on, wid hot
wather an' could wather, an' I kep
churnin away, but befor, if I kep' churnin'
from that good day to this, the divil a sign
o' bit o' butther ever came on the churn.

Did'nt I tell ye, Billy, says me mother,
that that woman was'nt lucky to crass the
thrassel this mornin. Ye may rise early to
morra mornin, says she, an' go straight to
Moll Anthony, says she.

So befor, I riz early the next mornin an' put the saddle on the mare an' off wid me to the Red Hills o' Kildare to Moll Anthony. Whin I came to the house, I met Moll in the yard. Me young man, says she, to me, suddent like, I know yer business, says she. Yer butther is gone. Befor, it is Maam says I, frightened like.

Well go home now, says she, an' put the plough irons around the churn, an' redden the colther in the fire says she, an' the wan that's takin yer butther will come roarin to the doore, says she. So before, I made no delay but come on home an' tould me mother what she said like.

Well, that same evenin', we prepared the churn, as Moll bid us, an' as soon as the colther was red, in the fire, a neighbour, that we never suspected, come roarin' to the doore, afther scaldin' herself wid bilin wather.

Me mother made for a kittle o' biling wather that was on the fire to throw it on her to scald her betther, whin she run for her life, so she did. Sure twas she that sint the other oul damsel for the seed o' the fire, that May mornin'.

So, from that good day to this, we always had plenty o' butther but we never gave away the seed o' the fire on a May mornin', nor never will plaze God.[14]

O

A certain farmer named B— lived in North Carlow and kept six or eight cows. A workman of his lived in a cottage near him and kept one cow. No matter what precautions B— took, or how careful he was in the churning, he could get nothing but froth from his milk, while his workman was sending a large supply of butter to the market each week from his single cow. B— consulted his neighbours and was advised to go to the Red Hills and take the advice of Moll Anthony. He went and got the following advice – 'Next time you are churning put the chains of the plough around the churn; put the coulter of the plough in the fire, make it red hot and then plunge it into the churn when the butter should be

forming. At the same time keep the outer door locked and allow no person inside at your peril'. B— did as he was told and when the coulter was red-hot it was plunged into the milk. A dreadful roaring and yelling was heard outside, and the workman came rushing from the field, where he had been at work, and tried to burst in the door. However, he was kept outside and appeared to be in terrible agony until the churning was completed, when the normal quantity of butter was taken off the churn. After this the farmer got usual quantity of butter from his milk and the workman no longer had a large supply to send to market.[15]

P

A case in South Wicklow had a less pleasant termination. A farmer named J— believed that his butter was being taken and decided to pay a visit to Moll for advice. On his way to Kildare a storm suddenly arose, and the car on which J— was travelling was upset and tumbled into the ditch. However, no harm was done, but the poor man was so irritated that he cried out, 'Musha bad luck to you, Moll Anthony; why did I ever think of going near you?' He continued on his journey and on arriving at his destination Moll said to him, 'Indeed, Mr J—, you needn't have cursed Moll Anthony on your way here.' She gave him the same advice about the coulter and the plough chains, which he followed out to the letter. When the red-hot iron was plunged into the milk a knock came to the door, and on opening it J— found a cousin of his in the yard. He attacked the man and gave him a very severe threshing, and it took all the efforts of the friends of both parties to prevent a costly lawsuit for assault and battery. He never complained again about his butter being taken.[16]

Q

Moll Anthony was a witch doctor who lived in Allen about 30 years ago. She used various herbs to effect-cures, but it is said that she was also in communication with the devil. She often cast charms and spells over those whom she considered her enemies, or over those who injured her in any way either by word or deed.

Once a new parish priest came to Allen and soon after his arrival he denounced Moll. from the pulpit, on a certain Sunday during Mass. When he returned to his home he found his beautiful horse on the point of death. Needless to say he was startled, as the horse had been in the best of health only an hour before. The neighbours of course gathered round, and were able to explain the strange occurrences, knowing that the priest was abusing Moll, they adviced him to go to her and make friends with her. He tried every available cure, he sent for a vet surgeon, but he could not diagnose the disease. One thing was certain, however, that the horse was dying.

At length the parishioners succeeded in getting him to go to Moll. She received him rather coldly at first, but in the end she said, 'Your horse is cured go home, and in future let me alone, and I will leave you in peace'.

The priest returned to his home to find his valuable animal galloping backward and forward through the field quite normal and fully restored to health.[17]

R

On the side of a hill called Grange which lies about two miles in a southerly direction from Boston school stands a thatched farm house in which till about two years ago lived a woman named Mrs Gleeson. She was nick-named 'Moll Anthony'. She was a wonder worker with herbal remedies. On her death she left the cure to her son James. It is said she could tell a person's complaint by looking at him, and that when a stranger reached the door, she could tell if the cure were required for a man or for beast. The people from a great distance off had even greater belief in her than had the neighbours. They came from every county in

Ireland to her, one time, or another. Some superstitious people believed she was a witch. She was specially lucky in curing animals. She used to go to the Wicklow Mountains to gather the herbs. She boiled the herbs kept the water o burnt the boiled herbs. She kept the dried herbs and several vessels of liquid in a dairy or barn which was always locked. When the illness was explained to her she got a bottle, went off by herself and compounded the medicine. The present owner of the cure is not as good as she was. There's an old saying that says, 'every generation is weaker than the last'. The neighbours got cattle, horses, cows cured when all else failed. Her herb water is said to have cured pains, aches, paralysis, rheumatism, and ailments too numerous to mention.[18]

S

A woman named Mrs Leisson lived in the Hill of Grange a small hill situated about a mile from our school. She died about a year ago. She had a great cure which was given her by an ancestor. Her nephew John Kennedy has the cure now. People from all parts of Ireland sent to her for bottles. One time people from America sent to her for bottles. Mrs Leisson gathered some of her herbs in wet boggy lands, and occasionally she went to the Wicklow Mountains. She gathered them herself till within a year of her death. Then her nephew John Kennedy gathered them but she mixed the bottles herself. She mixed a bottle which cured paralysis. She had a rub for pains. She made an ointment which cured skin diseases. This ointment was made from herbs mixed with lard. She cured pains and sores in horses and cattle. Her home on the top of the hill was like a Dispensary on visiting day. She never pretended. One time a boy with a sore arm went to her. His trouble was due to faulty attention to a break when he was a child. Without hearing details, she at once told him she was powerless to help him. He came from the West of Ireland.[19]

Notes

ABBREVIATIONS

NFC   University College, Dublin, Folklore Department, National Folklore Collection
NFCS   National Folklore Collection Schools Manuscripts

1. INTRODUCTION

1 NFCS, 776, 371–372. All manuscript materials held by the Folklore Department at University College Dublin are cited as NFC [National Folklore Collection], volume number, page number.

2 Diarmuid Ó Giolláin, *Locating Irish folklore: tradition, modernity, identity* (Cork, 2000), p. 17.

3 Ó Giolláin argues: 'The end of tradition is based on the ideal notions of a past completely dominated by tradition and of a present and future completely antithetical to it.' Ó Giolláin, *Locating Irish folklore*, p. 173.

4 Patricia Lysaght, who has written the definitive book on banshee legends, records a similar observation based on the wide-reaching collection of legends and stories that she used for her study. Patricia Lysaght, *The banshee: the Irish supernatural death messenger* (Dublin, 1986), p. 219.

5 Lysaght, *The banshee*, pp 154–81.

6 Another example of this can be found in Seán Ó hEochaidh's collection of folktales. In this tale, a man once wronged by a friend in America is carried back to New York City on Samhain Eve by a fairy after he does 'the good people' a favour. He is able to get back all of the money that had been taken from him and more, buy his wife presents, and return to Ireland all in one night, thanks to the fairies' benevolence. Seán Ó hEochaidh, *Fairy legends from Donegal* (Dublin, 1977), pp 347–65.

7 Ó Giolláin, *Locating Irish folklore*, p. 4.

8 Similarly, Guy Beiner argues that folk history, as a part of folklore, is also a living discourse. Guy Beiner, *Remembering the Year of the French* (Madison, WI, 2006), p. 82.

9 John O'Donovan, in his letters accompanying his Ordnance Survey work for Kildare wrote that the county, 'was so Anglicized that little or nothing can be learned from the present pronunciation of the names, and the natives have no traditions among them which would throw any light upon ancient localities.' Con Costello, *Kildare: saints, soldiers and horses* (Naas, 1991), p. 535.

10 For this see Terry McDonough et al. (eds), *Uninhabited Ireland: Tara the M3 and public spaces in Galway* (Galway, 2007), p. 11.

11 M.M. Bakhtin, *The dialogic imagination* (Austin, TX, 1981), p. 84.

12 Lysaght, *The banshee*, p. 156.

13 Full texts of the stories discussed at length within this book are included in the Appendix. They are lettered in the order in which they are discussed within the book.

14 All three descriptions of the cave are very similar: 'It is surrounded by rocks and furze bushes; and has an entrance hole.' NFCS, 775, 449; 'It is of a round shape with rocks all around it.' NFCS, 775, 450; and 'It is a vast square cave under a rock with a small hole for an entrance.' NFCS, 775, 451.

15 NFCS, 775, 451.

16 Dáithí Ó hÓgáin, *The lore of Ireland: an encyclopedia of myth, legend and romance* (Cork, 2006), p. 459.

17 Walter Fitzgerald, 'County Kildare
   folk-lore: "Moll Anthony of the Red
   Hills"', *Journal of the County Kildare
   Archaeological Society*, 8:1 (1915), 76–79.
18 Gearóid Ó Crualaoich, *The book of the
   cailleach: stories of the wise-woman healer*
   (Cork, 2003).
19 12 from Co. Kildare, 5 from Co.
   Wicklow, 4 from Co. Laois, and 1 each
   from Cos Carlow and Clare.

2. FAIRY WOMAN

1 Fitzgerald, 'County Kildare folk-lore',
   78–9.
2 David J. Hufford, 'Beings without
   bodies: an experience-centered theory
   of the belief in spirits' in Barbara
   Walker (ed.), *Out of the ordinary: folklore
   and the super natural* (Utah, 1995), p. 20.
3 Angela Bourke, 'The virtual reality of
   Irish fairy legend' in Claire Connolly
   (ed.), *Theorizing Ireland* (New York,
   2003), p. 31.
4 NFCS, 774, 117.
5 Lady Speranza Wilde, *Ancient legends,
   mystic charms and superstitions of Ireland*
   (reprint New York, 2006); Lady Augusta
   Gregory, *Visions and beliefs in the west of
   Ireland* (reprint Gerrards Cross, Bucks.,
   1970); William Butler Yeats, *Fairy and
   folk tales of the Irish peasantry* (London,
   1888); W.Y. Evans Wentz, *The fairy faith
   in Celtic countries* (reprint Gerrards
   Cross, Bucks., 1999).
6 Gregory, *Visions and beliefs in the west of
   Ireland*, p. 153.
7 Because the information used for this
   examination of fairy belief was
   collected in a limited number of
   parishes, it is possible that fairy belief
   was not as persistent in other areas of
   Kildare. However, the parishes used for
   this study were not adjacent and
   represented both rural and urban
   communities, so it is likely that similar
   information could be collected from
   other areas. These three parishes were
   chosen for this examination of fairy
   belief because stories about Moll
   Anthony were also collected from them.
8 Hufford, 'Beings without bodies', p. 22.
9 William Wilde, *Irish popular superstitions*
   (reprint Dublin, 1979), pp 10–11.

10 Emmet Larkin labels this process as the
   'Devotional Revolution'. Emmet
   Larkin, 'The Devotional Revolution in
   Ireland, 1850–75', *American Historical
   Review*, 77:3 (June 1972), 625–52.
11 Dermot MacManus, *The middle
   kingdom: the faerie world of Ireland*
   (Gerrards Cross, Bucks., 1973), back
   cover.
12 MacManus, *The middle kingdom*, 15.
13 Revd John O'Hanlon, *Irish folk lore:
   traditions and superstitions of the country*
   (Dublin, 1870), p. 37.
14 Lady Wilde, *Ancient legends*, p. 125.
15 Katherine Mary Briggs, *The fairies in
   tradition and literature* (London, 1967),
   p. 142; Marie-Louise Sjoestedt, *Celtic
   gods and heroes* (reprint New York,
   2000), pp 1–13.
16 Briggs, *The fairies in tradition and
   literature*, p. 145. Also, Carol Silver
   describes a few other explanations for
   the origin of fairies: 'the semi-religious
   notion that the fairies were the spirits
   of unbaptized children was also
   widespread and popular. Only slightly
   less prevalent was the idea that they
   were spirits of "special" categories of
   the dead, those awaiting reincarnation,
   or those killed before their time, or
   those from long-dead, pagan, or extinct
   races.' Carole G. Silver, *Strange and secret
   peoples: fairies and Victorian consciousness*
   (Oxford, 1999), p. 36.
17 Briggs, *The fairies in tradition and literature*,
   p. 145.
18 Wentz, *The fairy faith in Celtic countries*,
   pp 31–84.
19 Bourke, 'The virtual reality of Irish
   fairy legend', p. 28.
20 Ibid., p. 31.
21 Of local interest, a schoolgirl from Naas
   reports on the idea of second-sight:
   'No person, born in the morning will
   see a spirit or know anything of the
   Fairy world. Those born at night have
   power over spirits and can, if they wish,
   know much of Fairyland.' NFCS, 776,
   384.
22 Lysaght, *The banshee*, p. 41.
23 Susan Stewart, *On longing: narratives of
   the miniature, the gigantic, the souvenir, the
   collection* (Durham, NC, 1993), p. 113.
24 Stewart, *On longing*, p. 111.

25 Lady Wilde, *Ancient legends*, pp 38–9.
26 For general information on fairies, see Robert Kirk's, *The secret commonwealth of elves, fauns and fairies: a study in folklore and psychical research* (London, 1893); Patrick Logan, *The old gods: the facts about Irish fairies* (Belfast, 1981); Carolyn White, *A history of Irish fairies* (Cork, 1976); Peter Narváez, (ed.), *The Good People: new fairylore essays* (New York, 1991). For banshees, see Patricia Lysaght, *The banshee.*
27 Nora Naughton, 'God and the Good People: folk belief in a traditional community', *Béaloideas*, 71(2003), 13–53, 37.
28 NFCS, 774, 175.
29 NFCS, 776, 384.
30 Logan, *The old gods*, pp 105–17.
31 O'Hanlon, *Irish folk lore*, p. 4.
32 Ibid., pp 60–3.
33 NFCS, 776, 369.
34 Lady Wilde, *Ancient legends*, p. 114.
35 NFCS, 775, 406.
36 Meda Ryan, *Biddy Early: the wise-woman of Clare* (Cork, 1991), p. 11.
37 Fitzgerald, 'County Kildare folk-lore', 76.
38 The two other versions can be found in Con Costello, *Kildare: saints, soldiers and horses,* and in *Ireland's Own,* 8 June 1946.
39 Fitzgerald, 'County Kildare folk-lore', 78.
40 Ibid., p. 79.
41 Appendix, D.
42 Naughton, 'God and the Good People', 43.
43 Ilana Harlow, 'Creating situations: practical jokes and the revival of the dead in Irish tradition', *Journal of American Folklore,* 110:436 (Spring, 1997), 142.
44 Bourke goes into some detail about the effectiveness of moral behaviour against the amoral actions of the fairies in Angela Bourke, 'Legless in London', *Éire-Ireland: Journal of Irish Studies* (Fall–Winter 2003).

3. APPLICATION OF FAIRY BELIEF

1 Ryan, *Biddy Early,* p. 11. Appendix, E.
2 NFCS, 776, 366. Appendix, F, G.
3 *Linum carthaticum* (*Lus na mBan Sí in Irish*), commonly known as fairy flax or purging flax, this white, star-like flower was used medicinally throughout the British Isles as a purgative as early as the late Bronze Age. It was also used in the Scottish Highlands as a cure for menstrual irregularities and in Ireland for urinary complaints. David E. Allen and Gabrielle Hatfield, *Medicinal plants in folk tradition: an ethnobotany of Britain and Ireland* (Cambridge, 2004), p. 172; Niall Mac Coitir, *Irish wild plants: myths, legends and folklore* (Cork, 2008), pp 258–9. As this does not include a cure for sore chests, it is likely that the field's name comes not from the existence there of this flower, but because of the belief that the fairies occupied the field and so gave healing properties to the plants growing there.
4 Susan Schoon Eberly, 'Fairies and the folklore of disability: changelings, hybrids and the solitary fairy', *Folklore,* 99:1 (1988), 58.
5 Patrick Logan, *Making the cure: a look at Irish folk medicine* (Dublin, 1972), p. 2. Logan also writes: 'It has been estimated that one quarter of the medical practice in Ireland today [1972] is done by people who are not on the Medical Register'. Logan, *Making the cure,* p. 1.
6 Seán Ó Súilleabháin in, Logan, *Making the cure,* p. x.
7 NFCS, 776, 382.
8 NFCS, 777, 142.
9 NFCS, 777, 196.
10 Peter W. Nolan interviewed four active healers in the late 1980s that demonstrate the different types of healers that existed, and most likely continue to practice to this day. Peter W. Nolan, 'Folk medicine in rural Ireland', *Folk Life: Journal of Ethnological Studies,* 27 (1988–9), 44–56, 50–4.
11 James Mooney, 'The medical mythology of Ireland', *Proceedings of the American Philosophical Society,* 24:125 (Jan.–June, 1887), 137.
12 Quack is a term often used in some parts of the west of Ireland to describe folk healers. Nolan, 'Folk medicine in rural Ireland', 45.
13 Another archetype in the storytelling tradition is the seventh son, or the seventh son of a seventh son, whose

birth position enabled him to heal.
Within Moll's community, faith in
seventh sons was expressed within the
Schools' Manuscript Collection. One
girl, Patricia Meade, wrote: 'The
seventh son of a seventh son cures all
diseases by the laying on of hands …
When a seventh son is born, if an
earthworm is put into the infant's hand
and kept there till it dies, the child will
have the power to charm away all
diseases.' NFCS, 776, 386, 392.
Therefore, these men were born with
the opportunity to become healers if
they performed a ritual.

14 O'Hanlon, *Irish folk lore*, pp 51–2.
15 Jeremiah Curtin, *Irish tales of the fairies
and the ghost world* (reprint New York,
2000), p. 52.
16 Lady Gregory devotes almost an entire
chapter of her book, *Visions and beliefs
in the west of Ireland*, to Biddy Early,
Gregory, *Visions and beliefs in the west of
Ireland*, pp 31–50. For more information
on her see Ryan's, *Biddy Early*, and
Lenihan's, *Biddy Early*.
17 Mooney, 'Medical mythology of
Ireland', 137.
18 Within the information collected on
folk medicine from the parishes surrounding Moll's home, there was only
one cure listed for an animal, while the
rest pertained to human sickness. Bridie
Heffernan reported: 'Blood wort cures
blood murrain in cattle. It is boiled in
new milk'. NFCS, 777, 195–196.
19 Logan, *Making the cure*.
20 NFCS, 777, 24.
21 Fitzgerald, 'County Kildare folk-lore', 76.
22 Logan, *The old gods*, p. 97.
23 Appendix, H.
24 *Ireland's Own*, 8 Dec. 1956.
25 Logan, *The old gods*, pp 98–9.
26 Mooney, 'Medical mythology of
Ireland', 142.
27 Patricia Meade, from Naas, writes: 'If a
child is fairy-struck give it a cup of
cold water in the name of Christ, and
make the Sign of the Cross over it.'
NFCS, 776, 391.
28 Joseph Meehan, 'The cure of elf-
shooting in the north-west of Ireland',
Folk-Lore, 17 (1906), 203.
29 Appendix, I.

30 Logan, *The old gods*, pp 100–1.
31 Mooney, 'Medical mythology of
Ireland, 148.
32 Appendix, J.
33 NFC, 36, 131.
34 Eberly, 'Fairies and the folklore of
disability'.
35 Perhaps the most famous fairy
changeling case is that of Bridget
Cleary, who was burned in 1895 by
members of her family. Bourke has
brought her story to prominence
through her book, *The burning of Bridget
Cleary*, which not only describes the
details of the case, but also brings to life
the social context that brought about
this awful turn of events.
36 Appendix, K, L.
37 NFC, 36, 178.
38 *Ireland's Own*, 5 Mar. 1955.
39 Ibid.
40 Mac Coiter, *Irish wild plants*.
41 Allen and Hatfield, *Medicinal plants in
folk tradition*.
42 NFCS, 776, 386.
43 NFCS, 777, 25.
44 NFCS, 776, 375.
45 Mac Coitir, *Irish wild plants*, pp 278–80
46 Meehan, 'The cure of elf-shooting', 207.
47 Mac Coitir, *Irish wild plants*, pp 94–100.
48 Ibid., p. 96.
49 NFCS, 776, 392.
50 Ryan, *Biddy Early*, p. 11.
51 Fitzgerald, 'County Kildare folk-lore', 76.
52 NFCS, 777, 141.
53 NFCS, 776, 385.
54 NFCS, 776, 383.
55 NFCS, 776, 378.
56 NFCS, 777, 142.
57 Appendix, J.
58 Appendix, M.
59 NFCS, 776, 378–379.
60 Fitzgerald, 'County Kildare folk-lore', 76.
61 Ryan, *Biddy Early*, p. 12; O'Hanlon,
Irish folk lore, p. 50.

4. POWERFUL WOMEN AND WOMEN OF
POWER

1 NFCS, 776, 406.
2 Nolan, 'Folk medicine in rural Ireland',
45.
3 Angela Bourke, 'Reading a woman's
death: colonial text and oral tradition in

19th-century Ireland', *Feminist Studies*, 21:3 (Autumn, 1995), 571.

4 Nancy Schmitz, 'An Irish wise-woman', *Journal of the Folklore Institute*, 14 (1977), 177.

5 Schmitz, 'An Irish wise-woman', 174.

6 The preceding statement, as well as the following descriptions of the *bean feasa*, is summarized from Gearóid Ó Crualaoich, 'Reading the *bean feasa*', *Folklore*, 116:1 (Apr. 2005), 37–51.

7 *Ireland's Own*, 14 Nov. 1936.

8 While Ó Crualaoich writes that wise-women are often itinerants, they do usually have a particular region with which they are associated.

9 Ó Crualaoich, 'Reading the *bean feasa*', 41.

10 Ó Crualaoich focused on wise-women legends mainly from the west and north of Ireland, and so did not use any material on Moll Anthony, and also excluded Biddy Early from his study. Ó Crualaoich, 'Reading the *bean feasa*', 40–1.

11 William Byrne, 81 years of age, Kilranlagh, Killégan, Co. Wicklow. NFC, 265, 543–545.

12 NFC, 265, 545 [my emphasis].

13 NFC, 265, 545.

14 Appendix, N, O, P.

15 NFC, 36, 145–150.

16 *Ireland's Own*, 22 June 1946.

17 Cara Delay, 'Confidantes or competitors? Women, priests, and conflict in post-Famine Ireland', *Éire-Ireland*, 40:1 & 2 (Spring/Summer 2005), 123.

18 Naughton, 'God and the Good People', 26.

19 Delay, 'Confidantes or competitors?', 112.

20 Pádraig Ó Héalaí, 'Priest versus healer: the legend of the priest's stricken horse', *Béaloideas*, 62–3 (1995), 186–7.

21 Ó Héalaí, 'Priest versus healer'.

22 Appendix, Q.

23 Timothy Corrigan Correll, 'Believers, sceptics, and charlatans: evidential rhetoric, the fairies, and fairy healers in Irish oral narrative and belief', *Folklore*, 116:1 (Apr. 2005), 2.

24 NFCS, 777, 190–192, 205–207; NFCS, 776, 352–353.

25 NFCS, 776, 348–351; NFCS, 777, 106, 190–192. For further information on the use of holy wells for healing in general see Patrick Logan, *The holy wells of Ireland* (Gerrards Cross, Bucks., 1980).

26 Schmitz, 'An Irish wise-woman', 173.

27 Ó Héalaí, 'Priest versus healer', 175.

28 O'Hanlon, *Irish folk lore*, p. 243.

29 Bob Curran, *A bewitched land: Ireland's witches* (Dublin, 2005).

30 Canon J. A. MacCulloch, 'The mingling of fairy and witch beliefs in sixteenth and seventeenth century Scotland', *Folklore*, 32:4 (Dec. 1921), 231.

31 Read writes of this: 'Fairy-lore and witch-lore have, moreover, been confused. People use the words "witch" and "bewitched" when speaking of fairies.' D.H. Moutray Read, 'Some characteristics of Irish folklore', *Folklore*, 27:3 (Sept., 1916), 252.

32 Emma Wilby, 'The witch's familiar and the fairy in early modern England and Scotland', *Folklore*, 111:2 (Oct. 2000), 285. Cunning-woman is a synonym for wise-woman that was used mostly in England and Scotland.

33 Toradh can also be translated as 'profit'.

34 It does not appear as if Moll was ever formally tried with witchcraft, however.

35 NFCS, 776, 406.

36 One of the tellers asserts: 'This is the truth I'm telling ye, for she has a son abroad there today, by name Jack', Ryan, *Biddy Early*, p. 11.

37 Ó Crualaoich, 'Reading the bean feasa', 38.

38 *Ireland's Own*, 14 Nov. 1936.

39 *Ireland's Own*, 22 June 1946.

40 *Ireland's Own*, 22 June 1946.

41 Fitzgerald, 'County Kildare folk-lore', 78.

42 Ibid., p. 78.

43 O'Hanlon, *Irish folk lore*, p. 49.

44 Fitzgerald, 'County Kildare folk-lore', 78–9.

45 Ryan, *Biddy Early*, pp 11–12.

46 Ibid., p. 11.

47 Fitzgerald, 'County Kildare folk-lore', 78.

48 Appendix, R, S.

49 NFCS, 778, 196.

50 NFCS, 777, 169.

51 NFCS, 777, 131–132.

52 Fitzgerald, 'County Kildare folk-lore', 78.
53 *Ireland's Own*, 8 Dec. 1956 [my emphasis].
54 NFCS, 775, 450.
55 Fitzgerald, 'County Kildare folk-lore', 76.
56 Ibid.
57 NFC, 36, 148.
58 NFC, 36, 197–200.
59 *Ireland's Own*, 22 June 1946.
60 O'Hanlon, Irish folk lore, p. 49.
61 NFC, 36, 130–133.
62 Ó Crualaoich, *The book of the cailleach*.
63 Gearóid Ó Crualaoich, 'Non-sovereignty queen aspects of the Otherworld female in Irish hag legends: the case of the Cailleach Bhéarra', *Béaloideas*, 62–3 (1994–5), 150.
64 Ó Crualaoich, 'Non-sovereignty queen', 151–60. As Ó Crualoich suggests, the bean feasa is a human reflection of the cailleach. It is in this way that Moll's character absorbs and takes the form of the hag goddess, one of her many layers.
65 Smyth writes: 'Often translated as "an old hag"; however, an aspect of the cailleach is that she can change from that state to being a young woman'. Smyth, *A guide to Irish mythology*, p. 31.
66 Smyth, *A guide to Irish mythology*, pp 28–9.
67 Ibid., p. 29.
68 Ó hÓgáin, *The lore of Ireland*, p. 51.
69 Sjoestedt, *Celtic gods and heroes*, p. 24.
70 Ibid., pp 25–6.
71 Ibid., p. 37. Ó Crualaoich supports this argument: Ó Crualaoich, *The book of the cailleach*, p. 27.
72 Sjoestedt, *Celtic gods and heroes*, p. 18.
73 Hilda Ellis Davidson, 'Milk and the northern goddess' in Sandra Billington and Miranda Green (eds), *The concept of the goddess* (London, 1996), p. 91.
74 Davidson, 'Milk and the northern goddess', p. 99.
75 Monaghan, *The red-haired girl from the bog*, p. 168.
76 Davidson, 'Milk and the northern goddess', p. 100; Ó hÓgáin, *The lore of Ireland*, p. 58.
77 Thomas Francis O'Rahilly, *Early Irish history and mythology* (reprint Dublin, 1984), p. 3.
78 Edward Gwynn, *The Metrical Dindshenchas* (reprint 5 parts, Dublin, 1991), part iii, pp 31, 37; O'Rahilly, *Early Irish history and mythology*, p. 516.
79 Both Bóand and Bó Finne have been translated as 'white cow'. However, just as with Bouvinda, 'white' could also be 'bright', 'shining', or 'wise' in the case of Bóand. Monaghan, *The red-haired girl from the bog*, p. 184.
80 Ibid., 169.
81 Ibid., 183.
82 Sjoestedt, *Celtic gods and heroes*, p. 26.

5. CONCLUSION

1 Wilde, *Irish popular superstitions*, p. 20.

APPENDIX

1   IFC, 775, 449.
2   IFC, 775, 450.
3   IFC, 775, 451.
4   Fitzgerald, 'County Kildare folk-lore', 78–9.
5   Ryan, *Biddy Early*, pp 11–12.
6   IFC, 776, 397.
7   IFC, 776, 366.
8   *Ireland's Own*, 8 Dec. 1956.
9   IFC, 776, 381.
10 IFC, 36, 130–133.
11 IFC, 36, 178–180.
12 *Ireland's Own*, 5 Mar. 1955.
13 *Ireland's Own*, 22 June 1946.
14 IFC, 36, 145–150.
15 *Ireland's Own*, 22 June 1946.
16 *Ireland's Own*, 22 June 1946.
17 IFC, 776, 406–407.
18 IFC, 777, 131–132.
19 IFC, 777, 169.